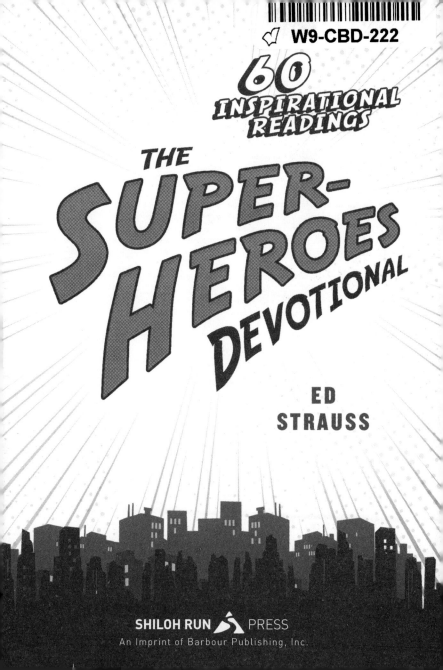

60 INSPIRATIONAL READINGS

THE SUPER-HEROES DEVOTIONAL

ED STRAUSS

SHILOH RUN PRESS
An Imprint of Barbour Publishing, Inc.

Print ISBN 978-1-63409-963-9

eBook Editions:
Adobe Digital Edition (.epub) 978-1-68322-302-3
Kindle and MobiPocket Edition (.prc) 978-1-68322-306-1

Cover Design: Kirk DouPonce, DogEared Design

Published by Shiloh Run Press, an imprint of Barbour Publishing, Inc., P.O. Box 719, Uhrichsville, Ohio 44683, www.barbourbooks.com

Our mission is to publish and distribute inspirational products offering exceptional value and biblical encouragement to the masses.

 Member of the
Evangelical Christian
Publishers Association

Printed in the United States of America.

CONTENTS

Introduction: Tale of a True Believer 9

1. God in the Comicbooks 15
2. The Infinity Stones 21
3. Being Extraordinary 25
4. The Rejected Hero 31
5. Our Incredible Armor 37
6. Calming the Monster 41
7. Legends of Gods 47
8. Heroes and Moral Relativism 51
9. Avengers and Defenders 55
10. Going It Alone 59
11. Hitting the Mark 63
12. The Hydra Conspiracy 67
13. Rising up with Wings 71
14. The Day of Small Things 75

15. Who Is Worthy? 79
16. Living in a Hostile World. 83
17. Removing All Restraint 87
18. Power at Your Command. 91
19. A Savage Antihero 95
20. Blending In 101
21. Escaping in a Heartbeat. 107
22. The Mark of the Beast 111
23. Superheroes or Vigilantes? 117
24. The Power of Forgiveness 123
25. Wisdom Versus Strength 129
26. Things Visible and Invisible 133
27. Hot Heads and Pride 139
28. It's Clobbering Time. 145
29. A Tender Conscience 151
30. Seeing Things Differently 155
31. The Great Power of God 159
32. Undoing Past Mistakes 165
33. An Imperfect Messiah 169
34. Overwhelmed by the World 175
35. Winners and Losers 181
36. Rising to the Occasion. 187
37. Respect for Divine Power 193
38. Super but No Hero 197
39. Seeking Revenge. 203
40. Attitudes and Prayer 207
41. Beware What You Think 213
42. Deadly Theology 219
43. Disunity and Civil War 223
44. Immortal Warriors. 229

45. Above This Dark World 235
46. Defying the Devil 241
47. False Gods and Christs 247
48. Overcoming Demons 253
49. Programming and Compassion 259
50. On Earth for a Reason 263
51. Overcoming Fear 267
52. Amazons of God 271
53. Running the Race 277
54. Decent Men in an Indecent Time 281
55. Beauty Is Skin Deep 285
56. A Chosen Ringbearer 289
57. Strength to Overcome 293
58. Emulating the Best 297
59. Hope and Justice 303
60. Are You a True Believer? 307

INTRODUCTION

TALE OF A TRUE BELIEVER

I'm a longtime comicbook fan. In the summer of 1962, when I was nine years old, someone who had money to buy things—comicbooks cost 12 cents each—trotted up our driveway to where I was in the backyard, bringing an issue of *Amazing Fantasy* featuring Spider-Man's origin story. I remember exactly where I was standing as I held it and read it from cover to cover, utterly fascinated. (I agree with Stan Lee, who insists that "comic book" should be spelled "comicbook" to make it clear you're not simply talking about a humorous magazine.)

Over the years I continued following Spidey's adventures, though I also read every Superman and Batman comic I could get my hands on. And when I started earning money,

I began collecting Spider-Man comics in earnest—even though the price had soared to 25 cents apiece. I soon realized that Marvel had a whole slew of other superheroes so I began buying every issue I could. By the time I was seventeen, I had no room left for clothes in my dresser. All the drawers were full of comicbooks.

I dreamed of working for Marvel Comics and I once wrote a letter to the editor suggesting a new story. Sometime later, I received a letter from Stan Lee himself, informing me that although my idea had him "on the edge of his seat," unfortunately, they weren't allowed to accept story ideas from fans. I suspect now that it was a form letter, but I remained a die-hard fan. I never ended up at Marvel, but I still was, as Marvel put it, a "True Believer."

Best of all, a few comics in particular helped prepare me to become a Christian when I was seventeen. Then I was a True Believer in the literal sense of the word. If it seems astonishing that fictional superheroes contributed to me putting my faith in the one true God and Jesus Christ, His Son, remember that comics are literature, an oft-disparaged media form that frequently just entertains—and often fails to do even that— but which sometimes carries deep spiritual truths.

Make no mistake about it: *many* comicbooks are insipid, contain over-sexualized imagery and gratuitous violence, promote unchristian values, and are a waste of time. . . just like your mother says. Certain stories influenced me negatively. And these days, the power of comicbook characters to influence us for good or ill has increased dramatically, since superheroes have leaped off the printed page into big-screen movies seen by millions.

You may wonder, "Can you actually find spiritual truths in comicbooks and superhero movies?" Yes indeed, along with much error. Superhero movies captivate people's imaginations with heart-pounding adventures, riveting plots, and spectacular special effects—and sometimes they have profound messages woven into them. Often the underlying themes reveal a Judeo-Christian influence and, even when it isn't intentional, you can still draw good messages from them, which is my goal in this devotional.

The apostle Paul was fluent in the culture of his day and often cited Greek poets, philosophers, and playwrights to make his point and communicate with his listeners. For example, Paul quoted the Cretan poet Epimenides in Titus 1:12 and referenced both Epimenides and the Cilician poet, Aratus, in Acts 17:28. And in 1 Corinthians 15:33, he quoted a zinger from *Thais*, a popular comedy about a prostitute, written by the Greek playwright Menander.

The Roman theaters of Paul's day were the equivalents of today's Imax cinemas, and if Paul were alive right now, he wouldn't hesitate to quote from *The Man of Steel*, *The X-Men*, or even *Guardians of the Galaxy* if they helped him drive home a message. That is, in fact, what I have attempted to do, and why I've written this devotional. I pray that these readings based on today's most popular superheroes and superheroines will both inspire and challenge you.

Ed Strauss

CANON-COMICS OR CINEMA?

A word about canon, the accepted lore against which all new stories are measured: While it's a given that the authentic canon for the superheroes' adventures are the comics, this book's primary intended audience is not superhero fanatics and collectors immersed in all the trivia of their favorite heroes, but for you, the general public, who may never have read the original comicbook adventures. The movies are often the only point of reference you have. Therefore, I also quote from the movies as authoritative.

Sometimes, however, a character's history diverges wildly between the comicbooks and the movies. For example, in the printed pages, Mystique was Nightcrawler's mother. Yet when they met in the second X-Men movie, they didn't know each other and were apparently not even related. When commenting on the *Captain America: Civil War* trailer, director Joe Russo explained, "We don't always honor the mythology from the books. One, because it's predictable and two, it's not servicing the story in the way we want."[1]

And which film version are we to follow if a superhero

movie series has been rebooted? For example, the three Spiderman movies by Sam Raimi (2002–07) and the two movies by Marc Webb (2012–2014), are all good, although fans have their favorites. And in the case of Superman, while the four movies starring Christopher Reeve (1978–87) are established classics and were blockbusters in their day, the movie *Man of Steel* (2013), with Henry Cavill as Superman, is also powerful and authoritative.

Some movies, however, were so poorly done that fans long to bury them. This includes *Hulk* by Ang Lee, the reboot of *Fantastic Four* by Josh Trank, and *Catwoman*. And while the first two X-Men movies are good, the third film, *X-Men: Last Stand*, was hated by many, and killed off or misrepresented numerous core characters, necessitating the drastic reboot *Days of Future Past*.

As you can see, the cinematic canon is in a rather fluid state—similar to the Aether, which refuses to remain in solid form like the other Infinity Stones—and while this may be a bothersome detail for some, it's what we've been given. So buckle up and prepare for the ride.

THE ONE-ABOVE-ALL

1. GOD IN THE COMICBOOKS

Many people have noticed that God is hardly ever mentioned in comicbooks. There are reasons for this. During the late 1940s, many comicbooks were filled with horror and gratuitous violence. As a result, in the early 1950s American psychiatrist Fredric Wertham led a crusade against comics, arguing that they incited juvenile delinquency. This was during the height of McCarthyism (1950–1956), so in 1954 the US Senate held televised hearings on comics' contribution to youth crime. Although a link wasn't established, the damage to the comicbook industry was done, causing a near collapse.

The Senate urged publishers to establish strict guidelines, so that year the Comics Code Authority (CCA) was created. All comics had to pass the CCA's censors to receive a stamp of approval. Among other things, the Code stated that "ridicule or attack on any religious. . .group is never permissible,"[2] and instructed writers to respect all beliefs and religious institutions. Publishers usually played it safe by avoiding the subject altogether.

Another factor was that until 1962, American public schools began their days with a short Bible reading and by reciting the Lord's Prayer. Then in 1962–63, the Supreme Court banned public prayer and Bible-reading from schools. Producers of comics, still smarting from the anti-comicbook hysteria of the 1950s, took their cue and usually didn't even give passing mention to a superhero's faith or the existence of God—not that many of them had been inclined to promote overt Christian messages prior to this.

They did delve into ancient Egyptian, Greek, and Norse gods, because those religions had long been retired to the realms of mythology. There had already been a number of superheroes based on Greek and Roman gods, so the Norse god Thor, which first appeared in 1962, was readily accepted. Writers also felt free to discuss the occult; hence the 1963 debut of the magician Doctor Strange was well-received. However, living faiths such as Judaism and Christianity were usually passed over in silence.

Any time a being identifiable as the Judeo-Christian

God *was* mentioned in the pages of a comicbook, you can be sure that it didn't happen without a great deal of thought. The writers had to really *want* to include it. As would be expected, the mentions were few and far between, but when assembled, they present a clear picture of the true God. This is especially true for Marvel comics. DC comics, while they depicted a being named "the Presence," have few unambiguous mentions.

In a 1968 issue of *Fantastic Four*, when her husband, Reed Richards, was in grave danger, Sue asks, "But what can he do. . .against the all-powerful Silver Surfer?" A Watcher, an ancient, wise being named Uatu, responds, "All-powerful? There is only one who deserves that name. And His only weapon. . .is love!"[3] This is the best possible description of God, since, as the apostle John tells us, "God is love" (1 John 4:8 KJV).

In April 1976, Marvel gave God a title when it introduced an omniscient, omnipresent, omnipotent Being called "the One-Above-All."[4] He was more powerful and exalted than any entity or god in the entire Marvel universe. Even the Norse god of thunder, Thor, was in awe of Him, calling Him "the Creator of all Universes."[5] The One-Above-All was responsible for the existence of all matter, energy, and life throughout every dimension.

At one point, a superhero named Adam Warlock told how he had been summoned to be judged by an entity called the Living Tribunal, who, great as he was, was "the servant of the One who is above even gods."[6] Yes, in the Marvel universe, the one true God is above the Watchers, the Elders of the Universe, the Celestials, the Elder gods, the gods of Asgard, the Vishanti, the Cosmic Entities, and even the Living Tribunal.

Now, the Cosmic Entities are eternal beings who wield power on an unimaginably vast scale and who are an integral part of the space-time continuum, essential to the running of the physical universe. The greatest Cosmic Entity is an omnipresent being named Eternity. But during one encounter, Eternity tells Doctor Strange that he and his fellow Entity, Death, comprised all the reality Doctor Strange knows, but adds, "Neither he nor I are God, for God rules all realities!"[7]

Around the turn of the twenty-first century, when the Comics Code became obsolete and the hesitation about mentioning Christianity relaxed, comicbook writers began drawing from its rich literature, lore, and symbols. This didn't mean the writers were Christians, though some were. But knowledge of Christianity still permeated Western society and people were familiar with its concepts. Thus, superheroes slowly began to be depicted praying to God, attending church, and fighting demons.

In the final analysis, we shouldn't criticize the comicbook industry too harshly for refraining from promoting belief in God. It's not their job to preach the Gospel. Jesus gave *that* task to us, His followers, and even many of us shy away from it. But it's great when comics at least give the one true God some long overdue recognition.

A colossal supervillain and a single overarching theme have been a part of many Marvel movies since *Iron Man* in 2008. That villain is Thanos, the Dark Lord—who featured prominently in *Guardians of the Galaxy* and briefly in *Avengers* and *Avengers: Age of Ultron*—and the theme is his relentless quest to possess the six Infinity Stones, also called Infinity Gems. The entire Marvel Universe is rushing toward the cataclysmic climax of this quest in the *Infinity War* movies of 2018 and 2019.

Thanos is a powerful cosmic warlord who reigns over an immense star-region and commands aliens called the Chitauri. In *Avengers* he allies with Loki to get the Space Stone, and in *Guardians of the Galaxy* he sends Ronan the Accuser to seize the Power Stone. Thanos wishes to woo a cosmic entity named

Mistress Death, and to do this he needs the Infinity Stones. (Thanos' own name is likely derived from Thanatos, a Greek god of death.)

There are six Infinity Stones. The Soul Gem enables its owner to steal souls; whoever masters it can control all life in the universe. The Time Gem grants control over the past, present, and future, and can bequeath omniscience. The Space Gem lets its user exist everywhere at once; it can grant omnipresence. The Mind Gem enhances one's mental powers, enabling that person to access the thoughts of others. The Reality Gem lets people fulfill all their wishes, even if those wishes contradict the laws of science. The Power Gem taps into all energy in existence and increases the power of the other gems; it grants near-omnipotence. Whoever possesses all six stones becomes all-powerful, all-present, and all-knowing. These are the qualities of God Himself.

Unfortunately for Thanos, when he loans the Mind Stone to Loki to help seize the more potent Space Stone, Loki loses *both* stones. The Mind Stone ends up on the superhero Vision's forehead, and the Space Stone is put under guard in Asgard. And Ronan fails in his task to gain the Power Stone; it ends up in safekeeping on the planet Xandar. This is why Thanos finally says, "Fine, I'll do it myself."[8]

Where did the six Infinity Stones come from? As Taneleer Tivan, the archivist called the Collector, explains, "Before creation itself, there were six singularities, then the universe exploded into existence and the remnants of this system were forged into concentrated ingots. . .Infinity Stones."[9] This forging was done by the Cosmic Entities, eternal beings who wield power on an unimaginably vast scale.

In Marvel's comic series *The Infinity Gauntlet*, Thanos succeeds in collecting all six Stones and mounting them on his gauntlet—and this is likely how things will unfold in the movies. In the comics, once Thanos places the Gauntlet on his hand, making him omnipotent, he fulfills Mistress Death's wish by killing half the living beings in the universe. Ultimately, Thanos is defeated because, after achieving godlike power, he abandons his physical body to become one with the universe. At that point, his granddaughter Nebula pulls the Gauntlet from his physical hand, puts it on and undoes his massacre.

In his desire to be like God, in his love for death, and in his desire to slaughter half a universe full of sentient beings, Thanos showed himself to be like Satan, "the god of this age" (2 Corinthians 4:4 NKJV). . ."him who had the power of death, that is, the devil" (Hebrews 2:14 NKJV). There *is* already a demon in the Marvel Universe named Lucifer, but Thanos also matches the Scriptures' description well.

Isaiah declared, "How you are fallen from heaven, O Lucifer, son of the morning! . . . For you have said in your heart: 'I will ascend into heaven, I will exalt my throne above the stars of God. . .I will ascend above the heights of the clouds, I will be like the Most High'" (Isaiah 14:12–14 NKJV). Ezekiel added,

"You were in Eden, the garden of God; every precious stone was your covering: the sardius, topaz, and diamond, beryl, onyx, and jasper, sapphire, turquoise, and emerald with gold . . . . you were on the holy mountain of God; you walked back and forth in the midst of fiery stones. . . . And you sinned; therefore I cast you as a profane thing out of the mountain of God" (Ezekiel 28:13–14, 16 NKJV).

The devil may have been intent on being God, but the Lord stopped him short and cast him out of heaven. And even though the evil one is still trying to bring death upon all humanity, Jesus, the Son of God, constantly thwarts his plan by saving lost souls.

In the end, there is only *one* Stone worth seeking and that's the one who gives eternal life. Jesus is "the stone which the builders rejected," but who "has become the chief cornerstone" (Matthew 21:42 NKJV). Plus, Jesus said, "the kingdom of heaven is like a merchant seeking beautiful pearls, who, when he had found one pearl of great price, went and sold all that he had and bought it" (Matthew 13:45–46 NKJV). Have you found this stone?

CAPTAIN AMERICA

3. BEING EXTRAORDINARY

Captain America is one of the most famous comicbook superheroes—and one of the oldest. His career began in 1941, during an age of heroes when millions of Americans were called to war against the Axis powers, the Nazis and their allies, a great evil that threatened to engulf the world. Captain America (Steve Rogers) was the embodiment of a hero: courageous, patriotic, and self-sacrificial. An old-fashioned idealist with a wholesome Boy Scout moral outlook, he often appears out of step with modern society.

As the Second World War is raging, Steve Rogers wants to join the fight but is repeatedly rejected at enlistment centers because he is so short and scrawny. Then he catches the attention of Dr. Erskine, a scientist planning to conduct a super-soldier experiment, which involves injecting someone with a unique serum and exposing him to "vita-rays."

Colonel Phillips doesn't think Steve is the right man for the test, and he recommends a certain Private Hodge as the ideal soldier. But Dr. Erskine says, "I am looking for qualities beyond the physical."[10] Colonel Phillips unwittingly proves Erskine's point when he tosses a dummy grenade among some soldiers. To his surprise, while everyone else scatters, Steve, weak though he is, rushes forward and throws himself on the grenade to protect others.

Iron Man later quips that Steve Rogers is a laboratory experiment and that everything special about him comes out of a bottle.[11] But that wasn't true. Steve Rogers was special *before* he became powerful. He had great courage and a strong moral center long before his physical transformation.

After Steve comes out of the experiment taller and superbly muscled, a German assassin kills Erskine. The assassin then avoids interrogation by committing suicide with a cyanide capsule. Unfortunately, Erskine's blueprint for creating an army of super-soldiers dies with him, so Steve is the first and only one. He becomes known as Captain America and is often affectionately called "Cap." He goes on to do great exploits against the Nazis, particularly Hydra, their Deep Science Division.

Captain America's story is reminiscent of the heroes of faith in Hebrews 11: "Their weakness was turned to strength. They became strong in battle" (Hebrews 11:34 NLT). They were powerful in battle, but even more importantly, God saw to it that they were "strengthened with might by his Spirit in the inner man" (Ephesians 3:16 KJV).

Just as Dr. Erskine didn't want Private Hodge, God doesn't always want men with muscles to do His work. God delights in using the weak and the incapable to accomplish great things, and He often refuses to use the powerful, the proud, and the self-confident. Scripture says, "God has chosen the weak things of the world to put to shame the things which are mighty" (1 Corinthians 1:27 NKJV).

When God looks for someone to accomplish something extraordinary, He first examines the heart. His reasons are simple. He not only needs us to trust in Him to work *through* us, but He knows that solid moral character alone is a strong enough framework upon which He can build greatness. Dr. Erskine explained to Steve that the serum amplified all his qualities, so that good became great and bad became worse. This was why he was chosen.[12]

Even after Captain America became a living legend,

he didn't let it go to his head. He knew the feats he was now capable of, but he didn't have an exaggerated sense of self-confidence. So when Red Skull asks him what makes him so special, Cap replies, "Nothing. I'm just a kid from Brooklyn."[13] In saying this, he was speaking for the millions of ordinary people who, although they were nothing special on their own, became great in serving God and their country. Only people who realize that greatness comes from God can be used to accomplish great things.

Jeremiah prophesied, "Let not the mighty man glory in his might. . . But let him who glories glory in this, that he understands and knows Me, that I am the LORD" (Jeremiah 9:23–24 NKJV). Captain America was definitely a dedicated believer. He is Marvel's most outspoken Christian. When Natasha (Black Widow) refers to Thor and Loki as "gods," Cap gives his now-famous answer: "There's only one God, ma'am, and I'm pretty sure he doesn't dress like that."[14] And, as Thor pointed out, Cap went to church every Sunday.[15]

Not surprisingly, a number of individuals didn't like what Captain America stood for. The arch-villain Ultron mockingly referred to him as "God's righteous man."[16] And Loki, after transforming himself into a copy of Cap, said sarcastically, "I can feel the righteousness surging."[17]

Despite his critics, Captain America's moral strength, courage, self-sacrificial spirit, and strong Christian faith continued to define who he was through the years. They were what made him a true hero. And these attributes can make *you* a hero, too—a man or woman who can do not just heroic deeds that make headlines, but the quiet, unnoticed deeds of daily self-sacrifice that are the mark of every true champion.

4. THE REJECTED HERO

Spider-Man is Marvel's most iconic superhero. Yet when editor Stan Lee and artist Steve Ditko created the Wall Crawler in 1962, they *knew* they were going against people's expectations. A superhero who had continual money problems? Who wasn't able to get a date? Who had an elderly aunt doting over him? Besides, back then teenagers weren't superheroes. They were sidekicks of the *real* heroes. You know, like Robin to Batman.

For these very reasons, however, teens identified with Peter Parker. In the comics, and in the movies by Sam Raimi, Peter is the ultimate nerd—off the charts intelligent but weak, filled with feelings of inadequacy, plagued by loneliness, and excluded by the popular crowd.

Many Spider-Man fans were delighted at how well actor Tobey Maguire captured the real Peter Parker.

Compounding his feelings of isolation, Peter is an orphan, having been taken in by his uncle Ben and aunt May after his parents died. However, as Peter grows older, he has all the desires of a normal teenager: he wants to be accepted and appreciated; he wants to love and be loved. He is, in fact, enamored with a beautiful classmate, MJ (Mary Jane Watson). But she is the girlfriend of Flash Thompson, the school's top athlete and Peter knows he can't compete.

Then everything changes. In the movie version, while visiting a science display, Peter is bitten by a genetically altered spider. Soon he finds that his body is rippling with muscles and that he has astonishing new powers—so much so that he defeats Flash in a cafeteria fight. But Flash still wows Mary Jane with his new car, so Peter enters a wrestling match to win the $3,000 prize, buy a car, and impress MJ.

Peter's uncle Ben cautions him that having the power to defeat his opponents isn't enough, but that "with great power comes great responsibility."[18] Peter rejects this advice and after he wins the wrestling match, the promoter gives him $100, not $3,000. Peter is so upset that when the promoter is robbed moments later, he refuses to stop the thief.

But two things happen that force Peter through an internal metamorphosis: first, in a twist of fate, the escaped thief kills Peter's own uncle. Second, the Green Goblin begins terrorizing New York City. The Goblin urges Spider-Man to join him, but Spidey refuses and risks his life to rescue others and defeat the villain.

Samson in the Bible had superhuman powers as well. At first, like Spider-Man, Samson was immature. He was foolish in his infatuations, looked out only for himself, lived selfishly, and used his incredible strength to hurt others for his personal gain (Judges 14:18–15:8). Like Peter Parker, and like Samson, you too may often be tempted to use your abilities and influence to aggrandize yourself, win favor, and put down others. Part of you knows it's wrong, but it often takes a wake-up call to truly realize it.

Spidey's problems and feelings of rejection aren't limited to his personal life, by the way. Even though he frequently risks his life to save others—for which he hopes to be appreciated—he is treated like a criminal. This was largely due to newspaper editor J. J. Jameson insisting that the "Webslinger" is a menace to society. In the comics, Jameson's unrelenting tirade results in the FBI offering a reward for Spider-Man's capture.[19]

Meanwhile, heroes like Captain America are highly respected. When discussing Spider-Man's bad reputation, Cap says, "Maybe if I make a personal appeal to the president. . ."[20] Spider-Man is a hunted fugitive, yet Captain America has an "in" with the highest office in the land—not unlike Elisha, who once asked a lady, "Can we speak on your behalf to the king. . . ?" (2 Kings 4:13 NIV). That Spider-Man lacked such favor, given all that he had done for others, wasn't fair.

With his superhero persona deemed a criminal and his public persona regarded as a weak nerd, how did Peter endure this rejection? By knowing the truth—he knew he was doing good *and* he knew he had powers his critics could only dream of. It's the same with Christians today. "We ourselves are like fragile clay jars containing this great treasure. This makes it clear that our great power is from God, not from ourselves," the apostle Paul wrote (2 Corinthians 4:7 NLT). This power is the Spirit of God within you (Acts 1:8) and with that great power comes great responsibility.

Remember also, Jesus Himself knows what rejection is like. Despite the fact that He did nothing but good, the public spurned Him: "He came to his own people, and even they rejected him" (John 1:11 NLT). Jesus was the ultimate example of a righteous man who was rejected, falsely accused, and made to suffer the shameful death of a common criminal.

How do you stand strong when you feel maligned and rejected? By following these instructions from the writer of the Epistle to the Hebrews: "We do this by keeping our eyes on Jesus, the champion who initiates and perfects our faith. . . . Think of all the hostility he endured from sinful people; then you won't become weary and give up" (Hebrews 12:2–3 NLT).

IRON MAN

5. OUR INCREDIBLE ARMOR

Iron Man, in his distinct red and yellow suit of armor, was such a hit in the first *Iron Man* movie (2008) that Marvel soon produced more films in the series, plus featured him prominently in the *Avengers* adventures.

Much of Iron Man's popularity, however, is due not only to his high-tech powers, but to how well Robert Downey Jr. portrayed Iron Man's alter-ego, the billionaire playboy Tony Stark. Downey seemed perfect for the role. Stark had a problem with alcohol and Downey has struggled with drug addiction. In 2001, Downey faced his problem. He later explained in an interview, "I said, 'I don't think I can continue doing this.' And I reached out for help, and I ran with it."[21] That kind of resolve is something to admire.

In the Marvel universe, Tony Stark inherits Stark Industries from his father. Stark Industries is a major US defense contractor that also supplies weapons for SHIELD, an espionage and counter-terrorism agency. Stark is a genius, and his inventions and innovations are on the cutting edge of technology, but he has no superpowers. What makes him a superhero is his incredible suit of armor. It transforms him into Iron Man.

Iron Man's lightweight suit of armor, made out of a gold titanium alloy (*not* iron), is a powered exoskeleton, and as such, it allows him to perform feats of great strength. The jets in his boots enable him to fly. His suit protects him because it is bulletproof and can generate an energy shield. Iron Man's most famous, most-often-used offensive weapons are the repulsor rays he fires from the palms of his gauntlets and the lasers mounted in his fingertips, although he has other impressive weapons in his arsenal.

In the *Avengers* movies, Iron Man constantly makes digs at Captain America, prompting Cap to counter, "Big man in a suit of armor. Take that off, what are you?" Tony Stark glibly replies, "Genius, billionaire, playboy, philanthropist."[22] Elsewhere he candidly admits that he isn't hero material, referring to a laundry list of character defects and to all the mistakes he'd made.[23] Stark's defects included alcoholism, womanizing, and a flippant, self-centered attitude. In a SHIELD report, Natasha (the Black Widow) writes that he "displays textbook narcissism."[24]

As Christians, we too have an incredible suit of armor that not only protects us from our spiritual enemy, but also allows us to launch attacks against his dark realm. This is why Paul advises us, "Put on the whole armor of God, that you may be able to stand against the wiles of the devil. . . . Stand therefore, having girded your waist with truth, having put on the breastplate of righteousness, and having shod your feet with the preparation of the gospel of peace; above all, taking the shield of faith with which you will be able to quench all the fiery darts of the wicked one. And take the helmet of salvation, and the sword of the Spirit, which is the word of God" (Ephesians 6:11, 14–17 NKJV).

Our armor, however, doesn't consist of physical materials, nor is it powered by human technology. It's made of spiritual light and power, and to put it on we must first dispose of our sinful habits. As Paul wrote, "The night is far spent, the day is at hand. Therefore let us cast off the works of darkness, and let us put on the armor of light" (Romans 13:12 NKJV). Just two verses later, he explains exactly what he meant by "put on the armor." Paul wrote, "Put on the Lord Jesus Christ, and make no provision for the flesh, to fulfill its lusts" (vs. 14).

Colonel "Rhodey" Rhodes becomes the hero War Machine when he puts on a suit of Stark armor, but Stark himself is at times less than worthy of the power his technology grants him. Once, while drunk, Stark shows off for a gaggle of scantily-clad women, blasting wine bottles and a watermelon with his repulsor rays.[25] He is recklessly endangering the public, so War Machine confronts him, saying, "You don't deserve to wear one of these. Shut it down."[26]

Christians are not always worthy of their armor, either. Too often, we, like Stark, make provision for the flesh, and, like Stark, we often suffer the consequences. Wearing "works of darkness" means living in the energy of your flesh, following your natural desires, and giving in to temptation. On the other hand, wearing spiritual armor means walking in the power of the Spirit of Christ.

In order for God to use your spiritual armor to protect you, empower you, and enhance you, you must stay close to Him and "live a life worthy of the calling you have received" (Ephesians 4:1 NIV). After all, putting on the armor of God means being "clothed with power from on high" (Luke 24:49 NIV), being filled with "the Holy Spirit, whom God has given to those who obey him" (Acts 5:32 NIV). You're only wearing His spiritual armor when you love God and do your best to follow Him.

You might be asking yourself, "Is it really that simple?"

Yes, it's really that simple.

6. CALMING THE MONSTER

The first *Hulk* movie, directed by Ang Lee in 2003, didn't get rave reviews for a number of reasons—one of which was having Hulk fight giant mutant dogs, including, of all things, a poodle. Thankfully, the movie was rebooted in 2008, when it was directed by Louis Leterrier and titled *The Incredible Hulk*.

In Leterrier's version, Bruce Banner is a scientist working on an experiment in which he subjects himself to a dose of gamma radiation, which unexpectedly transforms him into a superhuman being called the Hulk. When calm, he remains Bruce Banner, brilliant scientist; but when he becomes angry, he is transformed into a green-skinned monster that causes great destruction. Anger is the source of Banner's power, but it also endangers the things he holds dearest.

In the comicbooks, Banner's conscience was tormented over his Jekyll-and-Hyde transformations. He was man of peace, but when he changed into the Hulk, he went berserk and wreaked absolute havoc. So Banner constantly sought ways to control himself. Eventually he found a way. The 2008 movie jumps two years later to Rocinaha in Brazil, where Banner lives hidden among the working-class poor, works in a bottling factory, and studies martial arts to help him control his anger. He is also in contact with a scientist, "Mr. Blue" (Samuel Sterns), who he hopes will find a cure for his condition.

All this time, Banner is a fugitive from the US military. General Ross hasn't given up hunting for him, and one day an accident in the factory where Banner works leads Ross and his commandos to him. After becoming angry and battering his pursuers, Hulk ends up back in America, where, as Banner, he gets in touch with his former girlfriend, Betty Ross.

Meanwhile, one of the commandos, Emil Blonsky, persuades General Ross to give him a gamma treatment so he can fight the Hulk. He later forces Sterns to give him an additional treatment, and the combination morphs him into a superhuman freak called the Abomination. Banner transforms into the Hulk, battles Blonsky, and is about to strangle him with a chain when, seeing Betty's shocked reaction, lets him go—proving that even in his enraged state, the Hulk can exert willpower to control his rage.

Of all the biblical heroes, Samson most closely resembles the Hulk. God had given Samson immense power, and, like Bruce Banner, Samson only received superhuman strength during emergencies. The Bible says, "Suddenly a young lion came roaring toward him. The Spirit of the LORD came powerfully upon him so that he tore the lion apart with his bare hands" (Judges 14:5–6 NIV). It also tells us, "Then the Spirit of the LORD came powerfully upon him. He went down to Ashkelon, [and] struck down thirty of their men" (14:19) and "The Spirit of the LORD came powerfully upon him. . . . Finding a fresh jawbone of a donkey, he grabbed it and struck down a thousand men" (15:14–15).

Samson often gave in to anger against his enemies. But in his case, God allowed it because He was seeking an occasion to confront the Philistines (Judges 14:4). But in most cases, "fools plunge ahead with reckless confidence" (Proverbs 14:16 NLT), and anger *doesn't* accomplish God's purposes. This is because "the wrath of man does not produce the righteousness of God" (James 1:20 NKJV). So we must always remember that it's a mistake to boast about how formidable we are when we become angry.

We all struggle with anger, and we can all benefit from techniques enabling us to manage it better. When an upset Betty shouts an obscenity at a motorist, Banner chides, "You know, I know a few techniques that could help you manage that anger very effectively."[27] The Bible also offers some very effective techniques to control anger, which is why it can tell readers to "cease from anger, and forsake wrath" (Psalm 37:8 KJV).

It's important to understand that anger is not wrong in and of itself. God Himself gets angry at times, but the difference between human anger and God's anger is that He becomes angry very slowly: "The LORD is compassionate and gracious, *slow to anger*, abounding in love" (Psalm 103:8 NIV, emphasis added).

Solomon wrote, "Do not be quickly provoked in your spirit" (Ecclesiastes 7:9 NIV). James added, "Let every man be. . .slow to wrath" (James 1:19 NKJV). In other words, exercise self-control and don't allow yourself to be easily provoked to anger. Whether or not you believe you can do it, God *expects* you to control your temper.

Self-control is one of the fruits of the Spirit (Galatians 5:22–23), meaning that when the Spirit of Christ lives in your heart, He gives you the power to be patient and to forsake wrath. It won't always be easy. It takes time and persistent effort to bring fruit to maturity, so you must reinforce the habit by continually, consciously choosing to be patient with others and to forsake anger, thereby putting into practice these instructions: "Get rid of all bitterness, rage and anger, brawling and slander, along with every form of malice. Be kind and compassionate to one another, forgiving each other, just as in Christ God forgave you" (Ephesians 4:31–32 NIV).

7. LEGENDS OF GODS

The ancient Vikings worshipped gods named Odin, Thor, and Loki, and they created many myths about their battles and adventures. The *Thor* movies draw from these legends.

In the opening scene of the 2011 film *Thor*, three scientists are in the New Mexico desert observing an unusual light phenomenon when a large maelstrom develops. They decide to head toward it in their van, but visibility suddenly drops and their vehicle slams into a muscular, blonde man. They are relieved to find him uninjured, but to their surprise, he claims to be Thor, the god of thunder.

A short while earlier in Asgard, a celestial realm that serves as home to the Norse gods, someone has attempted to steal a priceless artifact. The attack is thwarted and the intruders escape, but the Asgardians have reason to suspect that the Jötuns, the Frost Giants, are behind the incident. Thor wants to attack the Jötuns, but Odin forbids it, because they have a peace treaty with them. But Thor impetuously disobeys, gathering his friends and heading to the frost planet, Jötunheim. Soon they are battling King Laufey and his giants. Odin arrives, orders Thor to desist, and seeks to make peace. But Laufey declares that it is too late; they are now at war.

Back in Asgard, an angry Odin punishes Thor by stripping him of his power and banishing him to Earth to live as a mortal. He is even separated from his Hammer, Mjölnir. This was why Erik Selvig, one of the scientists, remarks that he doesn't believe that the blonde stranger is the god of thunder.[28] Natasha Romanoff, another one of the scientists, was more credulous, exclaiming, "These guys come from legend. They're basically gods."[29]

Though the Vikings had worshipped Thor and Loki as gods, today they would be seen as highly advanced extraterrestrial beings whose powers would be attributable to advanced technology. Thor concurred with this, explaining, "Your ancestors called it magic. . .but you call it science. I come from a land where they are one and the same."[30]

Loki, however, still craves obeisance. He arrogantly states, "I am a god," and commands a large crowd to kneel.[31]

He strikes his scepter on the ground, creating a shockwave, and the terrified people kneel.

It's noteworthy that in the movies, only the villains desired to be worshipped. Thor has a much more humble attitude and speaks in awe of the one true God and of himself as one of God's creations: "Even I, son of one of the mightiest of all gods, find it impossible to conceive of such levels of power! And 'tis a humbling thought to consider how much greater the Creator of all Universes must be than that of all of His creations combined!"[32] Likewise, Odin, the king of Asgard, is under no illusions that he or his sons are actually gods. When Loki argues that he had attempted to rule Earth as a god, just as Odin had, Odin rebukes him, saying, "We are not gods! We're born, we live, we die, just as humans do."[33]

In the comicbooks and movies, these so-called "gods" were actually powerful beings living in another realm and another dimension. This is not to say that the Greek or Norse gods actually existed, even as extraterrestrials. No character in Marvel's fictional universe actually exists. But it helps to have an explanation that allows you to enjoy the adventures of Thor without needing to subscribe to pagan myths. Despite mistaken claims about his identity, Thor was a very likeable fellow—noble, courageous, and humorous. And when he finally learned humility and obedience, his father Odin allowed him back into Asgard.

As Christians, we understand that the legends of the Norse gods are only that, legends, whereas the accounts of Jesus' life are based on solid historical facts. The apostle Peter wrote, "We were not making up clever stories when we told you about the powerful coming of our Lord Jesus Christ. We saw his majestic splendor with our own eyes" (2 Peter 1:16 NLT). There's a big difference between the authentic gospels and manmade myths.

Many people today deny the existence of God and insist that they're their *own* gods. But the Lord told the proud king of Tyre, "Will you still say before him who slays you, 'I am a god'? But you shall be a man, and not a god, in the hand of him who slays you" (Ezekiel 28:9 NKJV). God has the power of life and death, which is why Jesus advised, "Fear Him who is able to destroy both soul and body in hell" (Matthew 10:28 NKJV).

It's wise to have a clear idea of your own mortality and limitations, and to realize that there is one all-powerful God to whom you must one day give answer. Whether you're small, weak, and insignificant, or whether you have great power and influence, "you know that he who is both their Master and yours is in heaven, and there is no favoritism with him" (Ephesians 6:9 NIV).

BLACK WIDOW

8. HEROES AND MORAL RELATIVISM

Natasha Romanova (Black Widow), a highly trained, beautiful, intelligence operative, was born in the city of Stalingrad in the Soviet Union (now Russia). As a young girl, she was orphaned during the Nazi invasion of 1942. She loved her motherland and after the war she became a dedicated KGB agent who was an expert in espionage and the martial arts.

In the comicbooks, Natasha was sent to the US to infiltrate Stark Industries; she and Tony Stark dated, but the relationship ended when he learned she was a Soviet spy. Then she fought Iron Man, Stark's alter-ego. She later met the criminal Hawkeye and turned him against Iron Man. She fell in love with Hawkeye and when she began plotting to defect to America to be with him, the KGB had her gunned down. She survived the attack and went back to the US, where she joined the Avengers along with Hawkeye. She later became an agent of the spy organization SHIELD.

Not surprisingly, the movies rearrange these details. In *Iron Man 2*, Natasha is already an agent of SHIELD, and she infiltrates Stark Industries at the behest of Nick Fury.

Natasha had no equals as a secret agent. In the *Avengers* movie, she is tied to a chair and interrogated by members of a Russian mob. Meanwhile, she talks her interrogator into giving her information. Then one of the mob's phones rings. The call is for Natasha; SHIELD is calling her in. When she understands why she has to go, she begins battling the mob, still tied to her chair, and beats them all.

Natasha is strikingly similar to Jael, a Bible heroine. Jael's husband was a Kenite who was allied with Jabin, king of Canaan. One day, after the Israelites routed Jabin's army, his general, Sisera, escaped on foot. Seeing him coming, Jael said, "Come into my tent, sir. Come in. Don't be afraid." So he went inside, saying, "If anybody comes and asks you if there is anyone here, say no." Jael agreed. But when he fell asleep, she crept up to him with a hammer and tent peg and drove the peg through his temple, killing him. When the Israelites came by, Jael went out to meet them, saying, "Come, and I will show you the man you are looking for" (Judges 4:18, 20, 22 NLT).

Like Jael, Natasha switched loyalties from the side of

oppression to the side of freedom, and like Jael, she didn't hesitate to use subterfuge and physical violence to defeat her enemies. Deborah the prophetess praised Jael in a song, saying, "Most blessed of women be Jael, the wife of Heber the Kenite" (Judges 5:24 NIV). Deborah went on to sing her praises for another three verses.

Again like Jael, Natasha's actions sprang from a deep personal conviction. She knew that the oppressive Soviet Union and the evil organization Hydra were wrong. This is why she said that when she joined SHIELD, she was convinced that she was going straight.[34] But *how* she went about serving the right side—ruthless and without scruples —showed Natasha's lack of a moral compass. She was untroubled by ethical questions, which is why Nick Fury said, "Agent Romanoff is comfortable with everything."[35]

Natasha had been raised in the atheistic Soviet Union, so she grew up believing that there was no absolute truth. As she tells Captain America, "The truth is a matter of circumstances. It's not all things to all people all the time."[36] This kind of moral relativism went against everything Cap stood for, but it's a common outlook among people today.

The fact is, when it comes to God's Word, the truth *is* all things to all people all the time. Adultery, for example, was wrong before Moses, was wrong under the Mosaic Law, and is still wrong today. It's the same with stealing and murder. And Jesus is still the Savior of all people throughout all time.

He declared, "I am the way and the truth and the life. No one comes to the Father except through me" (John 14:6 NIV). This fact is eternally the same. It never changes, because, as the Bible states, "Jesus Christ is the same yesterday and today and forever" (Hebrews 13:8 NIV).

Natasha, the Black Widow, is an amazing heroine, but she needs to learn the truth about God and His Son. The Soviet Union began collapsing in 1988, and today 52 percent of Russians describe themselves as "somewhat religious," and 72 percent identify themselves as Orthodox Christians, though they don't all attend church. It's time that Natasha, like so many of her countrymen, had a spiritual awakening.

Natasha once confided, "I've got red in my ledger. I'd like to wipe it out."[37] She had killed many people for many reasons, and not always for a good cause, and the red in her ledger represented the blood on her hands. The problem was that no amount of good she did could erase this blood guiltiness. If only Natasha would turn to Jesus, she would discover He has paid her debt in full.

THE AVENGERS

9. AVENGERS AND DEFENDERS

The Avengers is arguably one of the most popular superhero movie series in cinematic history. The non-stop action, spellbinding plot, interpersonal rivalries, and rapid-fire (truly funny) humor made the first *Avengers* movie an instant fan favorite.

The action begins when Loki, Thor's half-brother, in his desire to rule Earth, makes a pact with Thanos, leader of an extraterrestrial race called the Chitauri. Thanos promises Loki that if he'd steal the Tesseract—an ancient cube housing the Space Stone—and use it to open a wormhole, he'd provide Loki with an army to conquer Earth. Loki does this, and in the movie's climax, a vortex opens above New York and the massive Chitauri war fleet swarms through.

As wave after wave of alien battleships pour down into the city, the Avengers battle relentlessly. At one point, Iron Man, with a Chitauri gunship hot on his tail, leads it directly into the maw of a Leviathan, an enormous mechanical monster. When Jarvis—the artificial intelligence of his computer—asks what he's planning, Iron Man replies, "Jarvis, have you heard the tale of Jonah?" Jarvis answers, "I wouldn't consider him a role model."[38] But Iron Man's ploy works. One by one, the Avengers take out the alien warships.

However, the Avengers are in real danger of being overwhelmed. In desperation, SHIELD fires a nuclear missile to wipe out a wide swath of Manhattan, including the superheroes, to stop the aliens. But Iron Man intercepts the missile and guides it through the wormhole, where it explodes, obliterating the Chitauri war fleet. Immediately, the Black Widow uses Loki's staff to shut down the Tesseract-generator, closing the wormhole.

This was the first battle of the hastily assembled group of superheroes called the Avengers. As Iron Man said, "The Avengers. That's what we call ourselves. . . 'Earth's Mightiest Heroes' type thing."[39]

But this begs the question: What *is* an avenger? Well, an avenger is a person who takes revenge for a wrong done. In the Bible this was deadly business.

Even before the Law of Moses, people belonged to

tightly knit tribes and clans. If you killed a member of another clan, it was the duty and right of his near relatives to hunt you down and avenge his blood. Even if you killed him by accident, the avenger came knocking on your door. This is why, without negating that pre-existing law, Moses designated cities in Israel to where those who had killed someone by accident could flee for refuge (see Numbers 35:9–28).

The New Testament placed further limitations on taking revenge. Paul said, "Beloved, do not avenge yourselves, but *rather* give place to wrath; for it is written, 'Vengeance *is* Mine, I will repay,' says the Lord" (Romans 12:19 NKJV). Jesus brought vengeance to an end, saying, "I tell you not to resist an evil person. But whoever slaps you on your right cheek, turn the other to him also" (Matthew 5:39 NKJV). In effect, He was saying to let go of *personal* offenses. But He wasn't throwing out the entire justice system—particularly for serious crimes. Remember, Jesus commended the widow who repeatedly insisted to a judge, "Avenge me of [my] adversary" (Luke 18:3 KJV). Also, Paul appealed to the legal system to defend his rights (Acts 16:36–39; 22:24–29).

The command to "not avenge yourselves" also doesn't preclude the need for a nation to bear arms to fight crime or to defend its borders. Paul wrote of Roman soldiers, "He is God's minister to you for good. But if you do evil, be afraid; for he does not bear the sword in vain; for he is God's minister, an avenger to execute wrath on him who practices evil" (Romans 13:4 NKJV). So there is still a need for avengers to dispense justice. They just need to be duly authorized, like the police, the armed forces, and the law courts are.

If you're not an avenger in one of those senses, leave the avenging to those who are—or to God, the ultimate Avenger. But even if you're *not* an avenger, you *are* called to be a defender. The Bible says, "Defend the weak and the fatherless; uphold the cause of the poor and the oppressed" (Psalm 82:3 NIV). There are many people today who need someone to care enough to look into their lives, see their need, and defend them.

Also, as a Christian, you're to "wage the good warfare" (1 Timothy 1:18 NKJV) and "fight the good fight of faith" (1 Timothy 6:12 KJV). You're not to do violence to your fellow man, as "our struggle is. . .against the rulers, against the authorities, against the powers of this dark world and against the spiritual forces of evil in the heavenly realms" (Ephesians 6:12 NIV). The NKJV says that our battle is "against spiritual hosts of wickedness." It's easy to see the parallel between the Chitauri and wicked spiritual hosts.

Are you fighting the good fight of faith? Are you waging a good warfare against wicked spiritual forces? Are you defending the weak and the oppressed? You can do this in even small ways, every day.

WAR MACHINE

10. GOING IT ALONE

Stark Industries was an American weapons designer that landed lucrative government contracts, and the main reason for its existence was to supply cutting-edge military hardware for use in defending the nation. Thus, when Tony Stark created the Iron Man exoskeleton/suit of armor and it proved to be highly effective in fighting terrorists and other enemy combatants, Congress tried to get him to share it with the nation's military.

Stark refused, saying, "You can forget it. I am Iron Man. The suit and I are one. . . . You can't have it."[40] He declared that he could do the entire job of defending America alone. Instead of duplicating his technology for many soldiers, he insisted that there could only be *one* Iron Man—him. At first,

Stark wasn't set just against the military using his Iron Man technology and helping protect the nation. He wasn't even willing to accept *one* person's help. James (Rhodey) Rhodes, a Colonel in the U.S. Air Force, tells him, "This lone gunslinger act is unnecessary...you don't have to do this alone!" but Stark replies, "Sorry, pal, but Iron Man doesn't have a sidekick."[41]

In the first *Iron Man* movie, Rhodes serves as the military's chief liaison to Stark Industries. By the second movie, he is under increasing pressure to persuade Stark to share his technology with the military. Rhodes finally gets his hands on the armor, almost by accident. One night, Stark is in his Iron Man suit, drunkenly endangering lives and Rhodey realizes that he has to step in, so he puts on a spare suit and orders Stark to stand down. Stark says, "You wanna be the War Machine, take your shot."[42]

In the ensuing fight, the two super-empowered men nearly destroy Tony's mansion—and War Machine is born. After the battle, Rhodes simply flies off in the Iron Man armor. He takes it to an Air Force base, where weapons designer Justin Hammer modifies it. Features such as the Ex-Wife missile are of inferior quality, and they fizzle during an actual crisis, so at first, War Machine seems like a poor copy of Iron Man.

In *Iron Man 3*, Rhodes's armor is painted red, white, and blue, and he tells Stark that he is now called Iron Patriot, since War Machine sounded too militaristic. Nevertheless, the name War Machine sticks. In *Avengers: Age of Ultron*, Rhodes appears in black and silver armor and is once again referred to as War Machine. He joins forces with the Avengers to defeat Ultron and later officially enters the band of superheroes, along with Vision, Falcon, and Scarlet Witch. War Machine would eventually distinguish himself from Iron Man, utilizing a different look and unique weapons—weapons that actually work.

It's not hard to guess what originally motivates Tony Stark to be so territorial with his technology. When he states, "I am Iron Man. The suit and I are one," he is admitting that it was all about ego. He wants to be the *one and only* Iron Man, even though that leaves the nation more vulnerable. An entire cadre of fighters transformed into super soldiers by his suits? No! When Iron Man saves the day, he wants to be the lone hero getting all the credit.

A Christian leader of the early church had Tony Stark's attitude. John wrote that "Diotrephes, who loves to have the preeminence. . .does not receive the brethren, and forbids those who wish to, putting them out of the church" (3 John 1:9–10 NKJV). Thankfully, not all Christian leaders are like Diotrephes and not all superheroes are glory hogs. And even Tony Stark eventually yielded to the idea of another armor-clad hero flying around. By the time the events in *Captain America: Civil War* transpire, Stark is desperate for help—and glad to have War Machine fighting beside him.

The great Bible heroes weren't set against others helping

them. When Jehu, general over the armies of Israel, fought against the followers of evil King Ahab, he gladly let other mighty warriors join him: "He met Jehonadab the son of Rechab, coming to meet him; and he greeted him and said to him, 'Is your heart right, as my heart is toward your heart?' And Jehonadab answered, 'It is.' Jehu said, 'If it is, give me your hand.' So he gave him his hand, and he took him up to him into the chariot" (2 Kings 10:15 NKJV).

Jehonadab had heard about the great battle Jehu was involved in, and he was coming to join him. Jehu's heart was open to his help, but he only had one question: "Are you wholeheartedly for me, just like I am for you?" When Jehonadab assured him that he was, Jehu immediately took his hand and pulled him up into his war machine—his iron chariot, the technological wonder of his day.

May we draw lessons from the folly of egotism and be willing to share the credit as we get the job done. As War Machine told Iron Man, we don't have to do this alone.

II. HITTING THE MARK

Like Tony Stark and Colonel James Rhodes, Clint Barton had no superpowers. As Hawkeye, his prowess resided entirely in his ability to shoot technologically enhanced arrows with a bow and pretty much always hit his target. We're not told who produced his high-tech arrows, but most of them seemed to have been tipped with explosive devices. It could be argued, therefore, that his bow was largely a glorified grenade launcher and, considering his accuracy, it was highly effective.

Even though he was the world's top archer, Hawkeye didn't think he had a lot to offer, or that he was in the same league as the other Avengers. In *Avengers: Age of Ultron*, he says disparagingly, "We're fighting an army of robots. And I have a bow and arrow."[43] But when he asks his wife,

Laura, if she thinks the Avengers need him, she replies, "I think they do. They're gods, and they need someone to keep them down to Earth."[44] That actually doesn't make a whole lot of sense, but it was sweet of her to say it.

In the comicbooks, Hawkeye and Natasha Romanoff once had a romantic relationship. This past emotional closeness is only hinted at in the movies and in the second *Avengers* movie, Hawkeye is shown to be a happily married man with children, with Natasha now merely a close family friend.

In the first *Avengers* movie, Thor's brother Loki sought the Space Stone, an Infinity Gem housed in a cosmic cube called the Tesseract. Physicist Dr. Erik Selvig is experimenting on it when it suddenly opens a wormhole, which Loki then comes through. A powerful arch-villain named Thanos had given Loki a scepter topped with a yellow gem called the Mind Stone; this allowed him to control people's thoughts. Using this scepter, Loki gains control over Dr. Selvig and Hawkeye, turning them into his unquestioning lackeys.

Eventually, Natasha frees Hawkeye from Loki's control. When he wonders aloud how many people he had killed while under Loki's spell, Natasha consoles him, "Don't do that to yourself, Clint. This is Loki. This is monsters and magic and nothing we were ever trained for."[45]

It was a little simplistic of Natasha to say that they were up against "monsters and magic." This Mind Stone had a rational explanation, even if you had to understand theoretical physics to grasp it. It was one of six Infinity Gems, fantastic singularities that existed before creation and were compressed into unbelievably powerful gemstones after the physical universe coalesced. Confronted with such a powerful object, a mortal like Hawkeye stood little chance of resisting its power. Even brilliant Dr. Selvig had succumbed.

That was a good enough answer within the context of the movie, but what about in real life? When you've been misled into sin or false teaching for years, you wonder why God allowed it to happen . . . but God isn't responsible. When you lust, you fall into sexual sin. When you have "itching ears," you seek those who teach false doctrine (see 2 Timothy 4:3–4 NKJV). The Bible tells us, "Let no one say when he is tempted, 'I am tempted by God'; for God cannot be tempted by evil, nor does He Himself tempt anyone. But each one is tempted when he is drawn away by his own desires" (James 1:13–14 NKJV). This means that we're usually led astray by our own selfish motives, lusts, lethargy, and desires for self-aggrandizement.

It's true that you can be led astray by clever deceivers. Some con artists, including religious manipulators and recruiters, have very polished repertoires and are highly skilled in tricking people. Some charlatans have learned how to conceal certain disturbing facts from you, and how to give you a smooth line to reel you in to religious bondage. That's why the Bible tells you to be discerning and to have your eyes open: "Be no more children, tossed to and fro, and carried about with every wind of doctrine, by the sleight of men, and cunning craftiness, whereby they lie in wait to deceive" (Ephesians 4:14 KJV).

The devil constantly seeks to lead you astray as well, but unlike the fictional Mind Stone, he's not irresistible. The Bible says, "Resist the devil and he *will flee* from you" (James 4:7 NKJV, emphasis added). The devil is sometimes able to lead people astray, to work his evil so that they are "taken captive by him to do his will." But there is always hope "that they may come to their senses and escape the snare of the devil" (2 Timothy 2:26 NKJV).

Interestingly, the Bible makes two archery-related references to going astray and getting off target. God said of the Israelites, "[They] turned back and acted unfaithfully like their fathers; they were turned aside like a deceitful bow" (Psalm 78:57 NKJV). Like a bow that has a defect and can't shoot straight, they had flaws built right into their nature. Also, the Greek word translated "sin" in Romans 3:23, and many other places in the Bible, literally means "to miss the mark."

Watch out for deceivers and manipulators! Stay on track serving God.

12. THE HYDRA CONSPIRACY

In the movie *Captain America: The Winter Soldier*, Nick Fury, the head of SHIELD, discovers a deadly global conspiracy just before the conspirators are ready to strike—and as the nail-biting plot unfolds, Captain America leads the fight to foil their sinister plans.

In the comicbooks, during WWII, Nick Fury was the leader of the Howling Commandos, who were constantly being sent on missions against the Nazis. After the war, he joined the CIA, then SHIELD, rising to become its leader. In the comic series *Nick Fury, Agent of SHIELD*, he was a lethal fighter, armed with cutting-edge technology that transformed him into a superhero. Fury worked tirelessly against the evil organization Hydra, with its goal of world domination and its motto, "Cut off its head, and two more will take its place!"

In the movie *Captain America: The Winter Soldier*, Fury becomes aware that Hydra has infiltrated SHIELD. This causes him to worry about launching the new program, Project Insight, which consists of helicarriers linked to spy satellites, designed to preemptively kill terrorists. Had Hydra gained control of this program, it could wipe out all opposition. This, it turns out, is Hydra's goal. They plan to create such chaos on Earth that the nations would gladly accept their domination if they restored order and peace.

When Fury becomes suspicious that Hydra had deeply infiltrated SHIELD, he sends Natasha on a covert side mission to download Hydra's computer data from a SHIELD ship. Espionage has always been a cat-and-mouse game, with double agents infiltrating enemy organizations in the murky, secretive world of deception and counter-deception. Fury is a master of the game. As Iron Man says, "He's a spy, Captain. He's *the* spy. His secrets have secrets."[46]

While some Christians have grown skeptical of claims that we're living in the end times, you merely have to look around you to know that this world presently exists on the precipice of catastrophe. And if, as many people believe, we're living in the last days and the establishment of the Antichrist's one-world government is imminent, then his people must already be engaged in a massive conspiracy to infiltrate and corrupt the world's societies. The forces of the Beast have to be at work, in fact, if the events in Revelation are to literally come to pass.

Read what the Bible says about the man in charge of bringing about the Beast's reign: "He deceives those who dwell on the earth. . . . And he causes all. . .to be given a mark on their right hand or on their forehead, and he provides that no one will be able to buy or to sell, except the one who has the mark" (Revelation 13:14, 16–17 NASB).

The fictional organization Hydra is a fitting representative of the Antichrist's army. In Greek myths, the Hydra was a many-headed water serpent. Each time you cut off one head, two more grew in its place. John describes the Antichrist, saying, "I saw a beast coming out of the sea. It had. . .seven heads" (Revelation 13:1 NIV). The Beast of Revelation 13, rising out of the water, is a dragon, yes, but more specifically it is a many-headed *Hydra*, a water-dragon!

If the Bible prophesies that a Hydra-like regime is destined to rule Earth, there's not much you can do to prevent it. But there *is* an area where you *can* make a difference. The apostle Timothy wrote that "the Spirit explicitly says that in later times some will fall away from the faith, paying attention to deceitful spirits and doctrines of demons" (1 Timothy 4:1 NASB). Many believers have had their thinking infiltrated by ungodly worldviews and are buying into teachings that corrupt the truth. They accept New Age philosophies, sexual immorality, and false doctrines that allow them to live selfishly.

It's not enough to be aware of deception in the church or the world at large; you must also look into your *own* heart and become aware of the many-headed deceptions infiltrating *your* life. And you can be misled by good things as well. For example, 1 Corinthians 13:1–3 warns that no matter how many good deeds you do, they're in vain if you don't love God and others. Paul wrote, "I fear, lest somehow, as the serpent deceived Eve by his craftiness, so your minds may be corrupted from the simplicity that is in Christ" (2 Corinthians 11:3 NKJV).

What is this "*simplicity* that is in Christ"? It is, as the NIV states, "your sincere and pure devotion to Christ." John wrote, "this is His commandment: that we should believe on the name of His Son Jesus Christ and love one another" (1 John 3:23 NKJV). Jesus Himself said, "'You shall love the LORD your God with all your heart, with all your soul, and with all your mind.' This is the first and great commandment. And the second is like it: 'You shall love your neighbor as yourself'" (Matthew 22:37–39 NKJV).

Whether or not you believe in end times conspiracies, don't let secondary issues define who you are. Keep your Christian faith simple by first and foremost living the most basic commandments.

FALCON

13. RISING UP WITH WINGS

One of the great surprises of *Captain America: The Winter Soldier* (2014) is meeting a new superhero—Sam Wilson, the Falcon. Anthony Mackie played him in the film, and he also appears in *Avengers: Age of Ultron* (2015), *Ant-Man* (2015), and *Captain America: Civil War* (2016). Falcon was Marvel Comics' first African-American superhero. The Black Panther preceded him, but though he was African, he wasn't American.

Falcon's origin story in the comicbooks is different from the one portrayed in the movies. That shouldn't surprise us, but it does create a little confusion. But both sources have this in common: Captain America was the first superhero to meet him. In the comics, Falcon appeared on a Caribbean island where his plane had crashed.[47] Together with Cap and an actual falcon named Redwing, he battled the Red Skull and some superannuated Nazis.

Sam Wilson originally came from Harlem, New York City, where his father was a well-known preacher. But when Sam was 16 he turned his back on his parents' faith and announced he wouldn't be joining the church. The next night, his father was killed trying to break up a fight and two years later, a mugger shot his mother. As a result, Sam became bitter at the world and was soon deeply involved in crime. His meeting with Captain America and getting a chance to become the Falcon, however, gave him a new lease on life. In the movies, Sam Wilson has no superpowers; he is simply a good fighter with a suit that enables him to fly.

In *The Winter Soldier*, Sam meets Cap when he and Natasha are on the run, pursued by agents of Hydra. Sam takes them in and tells them about his past rescue missions with the "Exo-7 Falcon" flight suit, so they snag him another set of wings, and soon he is fighting alongside them. This lightweight mechanical pack gives him great lifting power. He is even able to carry Captain America through the air, though he complains that Cap is heavy. Cap jokingly replies, "I had a big breakfast."[48]

Like Sam Wilson, many people today were raised in Christian homes and have often heard the Gospel, but they have never received it. Jesus talked about this, saying, "A farmer went out to plant some seeds. . . . some seeds fell on a footpath, and the birds came and ate them" (Matthew 13:3–4 NLT). Jesus explained, "The seed that fell on the footpath represents those who hear the message about the Kingdom and don't understand it. Then the evil one comes and snatches away the seed" (vs. 19). A footpath is typically trampled hard by many feet, so seeds aren't able to sink down into it.

This scenario happens when you "harden your heart," so the Bible says, "Today, if you hear his voice, do not harden your hearts" (Hebrews 4:7 NIV). Instead, you are to listen to God's voice and draw life from His Spirit. Jesus said, "The words that I speak unto you, they are spirit, and they are life" (John 6:63 KJV). And Isaiah promised, "Those who wait on the LORD shall renew their strength; they shall mount up with wings like eagles" (Isaiah 40:31 NKJV). This beautiful imagery of lifting off the Earth and into the heavens captures man's eternal dream of flight and reveals why we love flying superheroes so much.

There are other winged superheroes in Marvel's Universe: Nighthawk, Darkhawk, the Wasp, and X-Men's Warren Worthington III (who went by the name Angel). In Warren's case, his superhumanly powerful wings grew directly out of his back.

The Bible describes actual winged beings such as cherubim and seraphim, and even two amazing flying women with the wings of storks (see Ezekiel 10:15–16; Isaiah 6:1–2; Zechariah 5:9). God Himself is likened to a magnificent bird of prey who, despite its fierceness and great power, tenderly nurtures its young: "As an eagle stirs up its nest, hovers over its young, spreading out its wings, taking them up, carrying them on its wings, so the LORD alone led him" (Deuteronomy 32:11–12 NKJV).

God is aware when tragedies and pain have wounded you and He longs for you to realize that He's watching over you and wants to breathe life into your spirit. Even when you're inclined to turn away from Him, He can reveal to you that faith in Him makes sense after all. As the apostle Paul explained his belief in God, the Roman governor Festus protested, "You are out of your mind, Paul! . . . Your great learning is driving you insane." But Paul replied, "I am not insane, most excellent Festus. . . . What I am saying is true and reasonable" (Acts 26:24–25 NIV).

Christianity is true and it is reasonable. Contrary to what some people think, you don't have to abandon reason and make a leap into darkness to believe in Jesus. Soften your heart and receive His Word, and you, too, can mount up with wings like eagles.

ANT-MAN

14. THE DAY OF SMALL THINGS

In the late twentieth century, scientist Hank Pym discovered groundbreaking technology that enabled him to shrink human beings to as small as insects—even down to microscopic size. He then designed two shrinking suits, one for himself and one for his wife, Janet van Dyne, and they became a crime-fighting duo known as Ant-Man and the Wasp. After many adventures, Pym was devastated when Janet gave her life while disabling a Soviet nuclear missile.

Then, in 1989, Pym discovered that the spy agency he worked for, SHIELD, was trying to replicate his shrinking technology. Imagine shrinking an entire army, complete with tanks, and smuggling it into enemy territory. Realizing how dangerous his technology was, Pym determined to bury it, and then he resigned from SHIELD. He started his own company, but even there, betrayal dogged him. Darren Cross, his young, unscrupulous partner, forced him out of the company and, copying Pym's technology, designed his own shrinking suit called the Yellowjacket. He planned to sell the suits to Hydra.

Desperate to destroy Cross's copycat research, Pym decided to enlist the services of former cat burglar Scott Lang. Lang had been sent to prison for acting like a modern Robin Hood, stealing money from a corrupt corporation and returning it to the people it had defrauded. Lang had just been released from prison and now longed to restore his relationship with his young daughter, Cassie. But he first needed to pay his ex-wife child support—and he was having difficulty finding and holding a job because of his criminal record.

Pym saw great potential in Lang and told him, "I've been watching you for a while, now. You're different. Now, don't let anyone tell you that you have nothing to offer."[49] But after several failed attempts to master the Ant-Man suit and its powers, Lang told Pym that he was the wrong person for the job. He not only felt like a failure as a father, but as a superhero.

In the Bible, a man named Gideon also felt like he had nothing to offer. The angel of the Lord appeared to him, saying, "Mighty hero, the LORD is with you!" (Judges 6:12 NLT). But Gideon couldn't see how God was with him. Then the angel said, "Go with the strength you have, and rescue

Israel from the Midianites. I am sending you!" (verse 14).

"But Lord," Gideon replied, "how can I rescue Israel? My clan is the weakest in the whole tribe of Manasseh, and I am the least in my entire family!" (verse 15). Like Saul after him, Gideon was "little in [his] own eyes" (1 Samuel 15:17 NASB).

God was determined to use Gideon and didn't give up on teaching him His ways, just as Hank Pym didn't give up on training Lang. To demonstrate that He didn't need vast forces to defeat the invaders, God shrank the size of Gideon's army—cutting it down from 32,000 soldiers to a mere 300 men. And God went on to use Gideon and his band to defeat the Midianites, just as Lang and his small band of friends took on Cross's organization and, in the end, defeated them.

Ants were Ant-Man's faithful helpers—hence his name—and the Bible also praises them, saying, "Go to the ant, O sluggard, observe her ways and be wise, which, having no chief, officer or ruler, prepares her food in the summer and gathers her provision in the harvest" (Proverbs 6:6–8 NASB; see also Proverbs 30:24–25). Lang, with help from his friends and a swarm of flying ants, took down the company's computers and planted explosives, which, after an emergency evacuation, were detonated. Most of the Hydra agents were killed in the ensuing battle between Lang and Cross, Pym succeeded in destroying the Yellowjacket research, and Lang's relationship with his daughter was restored.

The Bible asks, "Who has despised the day of small things?" (Zechariah 4:10 NKJV). The truth is that at times we all have. It would have been easy for Gideon to scoff at the thought that he could defeat a powerful enemy with only 300 men. After all, the Midianites "would come in like locusts for number, both they and their camels were innumerable; and they came into the land to devastate it" (Judges 6:5 NASB).

We too often think that what we have to offer is so small compared to the need that it's hopeless. Surely God could find somebody better, we think. But remember, when the prophet Samuel thought that the tall, muscular man standing before him was the one God had chosen, God told him, "Do not consider his appearance or his height, for I have rejected him. The LORD does not look at the things people look at. People look at the outward appearance, but the LORD looks at the heart" (1 Samuel 16:7 NIV).

If you think you're a failure, if you think you have nothing to offer, think again. God has been watching you for quite a while, and He's aware of potential you don't even realize you have.

VISION

15. WHO IS WORTHY?

In the movie *Avengers: The Age of Ultron*, a super-intelligence inhabits the Infinity Stone housed in the Tesseract, and Tony Stark and Bruce Banner seek to utilize it to create a shield around the Earth to prevent any repeats of the Chitauri invasion. While Stark's AI, Jarvis, is running the program, the Avengers are upstairs having a competition, attempting to lift Thor's hammer, Mjölnir. Suddenly, the super-intelligence, Ultron, eliminates Jarvis. Unknown to Ultron, however, Jarvis isn't "dead," but has gone into hiding on the Internet.

The Infinity Stones weren't evil in and of themselves. Only the Soul Stone seemed to have an intrinsically malignant nature. But Ultron had been corrupted by Tony Stark's sarcastic personality—and particularly his comment—

"Peace in our time,"[50] echoing British Prime Minister Neville Chamberlain's false assurance just before the planet descended into the horrors of World War II. This realization led Ultron to conclude that the only *true* way to bring peace on Earth was to rid the planet of violent humans.

Meanwhile, none of the Avengers are able to lift Mjölnir. Tony Stark theorizes that the Hammer is locked by some kind of personalized security code, but Thor replies, "Yes, well, that's a very, very interesting theory. I have a simpler one: you are not worthy."[51] Thor isn't necessarily being smug; very likely, he is remembering when, after first being sent to Earth, *he* himself had been unworthy.

Later in Seoul, South Korea, Ultron forces Dr. Helen Cho to use her synthetic-tissue technology, together with vibranium and the Mind Stone, to create a new body for him. However, as Ultron starts to upload himself into it, the Scarlet Witch stops him. Ultron is forced to retreat and the Avengers then take the inanimate body. Tony Stark can't resist completing his original quest, however, and when the other Avengers are away, he and Dr. Banner download the "good" AI, Jarvis, into the synthetic body.

The other Avengers show up before Stark can bring this creation to life and stop him. Then Thor arrives, whips up a lightning storm, and activates the body containing Jarvis' intelligence—and the superhero named Vision is born. He has superhuman strength and powers, but because he has the Mind Stone in his forehead, the Avengers doubt that he can be trusted. After all, he is empowered by one of the Infinity Stones, just like Ultron.

Vision says that although he can't convince them he is benign, they have to trust him if they are to stop Ultron. He then picks up Mjölnir, hands it to Thor, and says they need to get going. Astonishingly, he has just done what none of the Avengers had been able to do—lift Mjölnir—proving that he is *worthy*. Thor observes, "If he can wield the Hammer, he can keep the Stone."[52]

Then, together with the Avengers, Vision helps to destroy Ultron—blasting him with a powerful ray of energy emanating from the Infinity Stone on his forehead.

Thor states the reason the others hadn't been able to lift the Hammer: they weren't worthy. This is reminiscent of a scene that transpired in heaven. When the apostle John was before God's throne, he saw Him holding a great scroll, held shut with seven stamped seals, and he heard an angel ask, "Who is worthy to open the scroll and to loose its seals?" (Revelation 5:2 NKJV). However, no one in heaven or on the earth was able to open the scroll, or even to look at it. So John wept profusely "because no one was found worthy to open and read the scroll, or to look at it" (vs. 4).

Then Jesus took the scroll, and the twenty-four elders sang, "You are worthy to take the scroll, and to open its seals; for You were slain, and have redeemed us to God by

Your blood." Then John heard the heavenly hosts saying, "Worthy is the Lamb who was slain to receive power and riches and wisdom, and strength and honor and glory and blessing!" (vss. 9, 12).

No one else *was* able. Jesus, the Son of God, alone is worthy, and therefore He is the only one who can save you. The Son of God, "being the brightness of His glory and the express image of His person, and upholding all things by the word of His power, when He had by Himself purged our sins, sat down at the right hand of the Majesty on high" (Hebrews 1:2–3 NKJV). He alone could rightfully accept this glory and honor.

While Christians aren't worthy in themselves and can't save themselves, as believers, we *are* asked to walk in Jesus' footsteps: "He who says he abides in Him ought himself also to walk just as He walked" (1 John 2:6 NKJV). In *that* sense, we are called to be worthy. Paul said, "Walk worthy of God who calls you into His own kingdom and glory" (1 Thessalonians 2:12 NKJV). You do this by living in His Spirit, by being empowered by His love and goodness, and by looking to His super-intelligence to give you wisdom.

PROFESSOR X

16. LIVING IN A HOSTILE WORLD

Professor X (Charles Xavier) was a mutant with a strong telepathic gift that allowed him to not only read minds, but to control the thoughts of others. He frequently used this ability to locate and help other mutants. Realizing that they were misunderstood by their parents and feared, marginalized, and rejected by society, he founded a school called *Xavier's School for Gifted Youngsters*, where young mutants could study, as well as learn to control their powers.

Charles Xavier was a paraplegic, confined to a wheelchair most of the time. As a young man, he created a drug that reversed his condition and allowed him to walk, but because it shut down his telepathic abilities, he stopped taking it.

After Xavier's earliest students grew up, some became

teachers at his school. They also used their powers to defend the younger students from enemies, whether bigoted anti-mutant forces or violent mutants. These first students became known as the X-Men and they went on to defend the larger society, which often failed to appreciate their heroic, self-sacrificial efforts.

In the Marvel universe, mutants aren't a different species from homo sapiens. They're human beings whose genetic makeup is slightly divergent from normal humans, which often gives them unique powers and abilities and frequently causes them to look different from others. This usually caused people to fear them, speak evil of them, and persecute them. Magneto agitated for mutants to use their powers to fight humanity, but Xavier urged peaceful coexistence and nonviolent affirmation of mutant rights, to show the public that they had nothing to fear.

There are clear parallels in this for Christians. Paul wrote, "If it is possible, as far as it depends on you, live at peace with everyone" (Romans 12:18 NIV). Peter added, "Beloved, I urge you as aliens and strangers to. . . . Keep your behavior excellent among the Gentiles, so that in the thing in which they slander you as evildoers, they may because of your good deeds, as they observe them, glorify God. . . . Submit yourselves for the Lord's sake to every human institution [government]. . . . For such is the will of God that by doing right you may silence the ignorance of foolish men (1 Peter 2:11–13, 15 NASB). Like the mutants, Christians are often "aliens and strangers" in this world, set apart from others by their faith in Christ, by their unique outlook on issues, and by their different lifestyle. While most Christians in America may not be marginalized outcasts, in much of the rest of the world, this is definitely the case for believers. The past several years have seen the highest level of violent persecution against followers of Jesus in modern centuries, and it's becoming steadily worse. Some 100 million Christians are being persecuted worldwide right now, many suffering unprecedented levels of discrimination, exclusion, and violence. As Storm said, "We live in an age of darkness—a world full of fear, hate and intolerance."[53]

Though you probably don't have outstanding gifts that could be considered superpowers, as a believer you have God's Spirit living in you, giving you access to *His* unlimited power. And God has declared that He will answer your prayers and do miraculous things for you that you alone can't do: "We now have this light shining in our hearts, but we ourselves are like fragile clay jars containing this great treasure. This makes it clear that our great power is from God, not from ourselves" (2 Corinthians 4:7 NLT).

Speaking of prayer, Jesus commanded, "Love your enemies and pray for those who persecute you" (Matthew 5:44 NIV). You might have difficulty loving those who hate you, and you may wonder why you should bother praying for people who torment you. In the beginning, Logan asks a fellow mutant a similar question: "The whole world out there is full of people who hate and fear you, and you're wasting your time trying to protect them?"[54]

But you *should* love people and pray for them, whether or not you feel they deserve it. They may dislike you and look down on you because you're different, but it's precisely because you *are* different that you should love them. The Spirit of Jesus dwells in your heart and He makes the difference. In the words of the apostle Paul, "The love of God has been poured out in our hearts by the Holy Spirit who was given to us" (Romans 5:5 NKJV).

Charles Xavier observed, "Magneto doesn't share my respect for mankind."[55] Indeed he didn't! Magneto remarked, "We are the future, Charles, not them. They no longer matter."[56]

Some believers have a Magneto mindset: they realize that as Christians they're distinct from the rest of the world. But this then gives them the idea that they're *better* than others—just as Magneto boasted that mutants were superior to ordinary mortals. Some believers believe God favors only *them*, so they look down on unbelievers. This is the wrong attitude. God loves everyone in the world, and Jesus said that whoever wants to be first must be servant of all. Even Jesus Himself didn't come to be served, but to serve (see Mark 10:44–45).

JEAN GREY

17. REMOVING ALL RESTRAINT

Dr. Jean Grey was a calm, quiet, selfless member of the X-Men. As a mutant, she had some telepathic and telekinetic powers—the ability to move an object by merely thinking of it—but in the movie *X-Men 3: The Last Stand*, we learn that Jean has tremendous latent abilities to move and manipulate matter. In fact, as a young girl, her abilities were so off the charts that she didn't know how to control them. So when Charles Xavier takes her under his wing, he puts safeguards and controls in her mind to prevent her from accessing her full power.

At the end of the second *X-Men* movie, Jean sacrifices herself by leaving the X-Jet and creating a telekinetic wall to prevent the waters of a burst dam from sweeping over them.

She mentally activates the jet's malfunctioning vertical thrusters, allowing her friends to escape. She then collapses, releasing the rushing water, and apparently drowns in the process.

In the next movie, we are surprised to learn that Jean has not only survived, but has gone through a tremendous transformation. Her great exertion of power has swept away all Xavier's mental blocks, releasing her latent powers, and she morphs from the quiet, peaceful Jean Grey into the violent, lethal Dark Phoenix. Magneto is delighted to see Jean's full powers bloom, because he wants a powerful ally.

Magneto convinces Dark Phoenix that Xavier had only wanted to control and hold her back, and now, with all restraints gone, he tells her, "You, you can do anything—*anything* you can think of."[57] This is reminiscent of what the Bible says about humanity at the tower of Babel: "Now nothing which they purpose to do will be impossible for them" (Genesis 11:6 NASB). But like Dark Phoenix, mankind's purposes were predominantly destructive, since "every intent of the thoughts of [their] heart was only evil continually" (Genesis 6:5 NASB).

We're glad when we see a Marvel villain change for the better and choose to fight on the side of right. Think of Elektra, Black Widow, Quicksilver, or the Scarlet Witch, all of whom morphed from self-centered criminals and enemies into heroes. But it's very unsettling to watch a hero or heroine fall from a noble estate and go over to the dark side—destroying rather than protecting—which is what Jean did.

In the beginning of the movie, Xavier refers to the power each mutant has, then asks, "The question is: Will you control that power. . .or let it control you?"[58] In Jean's case, he realizes that her power is too *strong* for her to control—so he puts checks and safeguards in place. God has done the same thing for us. Paul wrote, "I have the desire to do what is good, but I cannot carry it out. For I do not do the good I want to do, but the evil I do not want to do—this I keep on doing" (Romans 7:18–19 NIV). God knows how strong our will and our selfish human nature can be, so He put moral commands in place, such as the Ten Commandments in Exodus and Jesus' commandments in the Sermon on the Mount, to direct our thoughts and actions. But you can't overcome by yourself. In Romans 7, Paul frankly admitted his inability to obey God's Law.

If you stay close to the Lord, constantly yield to His Spirit, and acknowledge the authority of His commands, He can strengthen you and protect you. However, if you willfully ignore His Word, you bring great harm to yourself and others. In the movie, Jean killed Cyclops, the man she loved, and destroyed Charles Xavier, her gentle mentor, while she was in the Dark Phoenix state. In her rage, she continued annihilating people until Wolverine slayed her.

This is an ongoing battle for all people: whether to yield to God's will and acknowledge Him as master, or to seek to assert their own will and set themselves up as a god. Adam and Eve tried to grab what was forbidden to them because the serpent told them it would make them like God. Magneto constantly appeals to this desire in people. He flatters Jean, asking, "Why would Charles want to turn this goddess into a mortal?"[59] He tells another mutant, Pyro, "You are a god among insects."[60]

In reality, human beings, no matter how powerful they are, are not gods: "'The terror you inspire and the pride of your heart have deceived you. . . . I will bring you down,' declares the LORD" (Jeremiah 49:16 NIV). Furthermore, their own lack of self-control will contribute greatly to their fall: "An evil man. . . . Will die for lack of self-control; he will be lost because of his great foolishness" (Proverbs 5:22–23 NLT).

In the end, even Magneto realizes his folly in helping unleash the Dark Phoenix, gasping, "What have I done?"[61] In a similar way, yielding to Dark Phoenix's destructive impulses brings chaos and disaster to individual lives, while relying on God to keep you faithful will guard you on your journey.

STORM

18. POWER AT YOUR COMMAND

One of the most outstanding X-Men is not a man at all, but a woman—a black woman—named Ororo Munroe, who goes by the name Storm. She's an amazing character with strong, admirable traits and has been part of the X-Men for many years. She's also one of the wisest mutants. Charles Xavier appointed Storm as leader of the X-Men in the third movie; then after he died, she proved to be both capable and confident.

While Jean Grey was caught up in a love triangle with Cyclops and Wolverine, Storm remained solitary. In the comics, she eventually married T'Challa, the Black Panther, yet for many years she remained single. Perhaps it was her serious, regal nature and often angry demeanor that discouraged romantic interest. As Nightcrawler observed, "Someone so beautiful should not be so angry."[62]

Not only was Storm beautiful and not only did she possess a commanding presence, but she had potent and far-ranging superpowers. She was able to control the weather over large areas, creating thunderstorms, lightning, tornadoes, blizzards, thick mists, or clear skies. Storm could also summon wind powerful enough to carry her aloft. Since her negative emotions could cause overcast skies or even extreme weather, she often suppressed her feelings.

Small wonder that Storm was a prominent member of the X-Men who was repeatedly called into the thick of the battle. It's always awesome to see her suspended in midair, her hair blowing wildly while dark clouds churn in the background, with bolts of lightning flashing around her. She makes a valuable ally and a formidable adversary.

In the comicbooks, when Storm was young and living in Africa, a display of her powers caused a local tribe to worship her as a goddess. A similar thing once happened to Paul and Barnabas (Acts 14:11–18). Fortunately, however, Storm didn't let it go to her head, but used her powers to fight evil, protect the vulnerable, and serve others.

In reality, only God has power over the weather: "This is what the Sovereign LORD says: In my wrath I will unleash a violent wind, and in my anger hailstones and torrents of rain will fall with destructive fury" (Ezekiel 13:13 NIV). Also read, "He shot his arrows and scattered the enemy, with great bolts of lightning he routed them" (Psalm 18:14 NIV). Elsewhere He refers to "storehouses of the hail, which I reserve for . . . days of war and battle" (Job 38:22–23 NIV).

God's Son also demonstrated His authority over the elements. One time Jesus and His disciples were crossing the Sea of Galilee when "a fierce storm came up." Jesus rebuked the wind, and it instantly stopped: "The disciples were absolutely terrified. 'Who is this man?' they asked each other. 'Even the wind and waves obey him!'" (Mark 4:37, 41 NLT).

And God will empower the two end time prophets to command plagues and control the weather at will. He says, "I will give power to my two witnesses. . . . These have power to shut heaven, so that no rain falls in the days of their prophecy . . . and to strike the earth with all plagues, *as often as they desire*" (Revelation 11:3, 6 NKJV, emphasis added).

Perhaps you desire this same power, not just to change the weather, but to make things happen at will. If we're honest with ourselves, we have to admit that we sometimes dislike petitioning God to act and then leaving the decision on how to answer our prayers in His hands. And even when He *does* answer, He frequently takes longer than we like. So we wish we could simply pray and have our requests answered instantly. . .and not just on rare occasions, but all the time.

But that's *not* usually the way prayer works. Believers are encouraged to present their prayer requests boldly before God's throne, but they're still requests, not demands. God is not a genie in a bottle, doing our bidding at our command. God is sovereign and answers prayer in different ways. Sometimes He says, "Yes," other times He says, "No," and quite often He says, "Wait—and *while* you're waiting, keep praying." Remember, even the great prophet Elijah had to pray earnestly and fervently concerning the weather, and he had to repeat his petitions seven times (1 Kings 18:42–44; James 5:16–18).

Quite often, however, when God delays in answering prayer, many Christians become discouraged. . .or they give in to bitterness and give up on praying altogether. They may then proceed to take matters into their own hands. Magneto had this mentality. In his opinion, "God works too slow."[63] Likewise, Abraham decided not to wait for God to fulfill the promise of a son, taking Hagar and producing Ishmael (see Genesis 16). But the Lord has good reasons for taking His time, which we often find out after nervously fretting about His delays.

Certainly, do your part. Do what God requires you to do. But beyond that, learn to wait on Him and trust Him to answer prayer in His way and in His time.

19. A SAVAGE ANTIHERO

Wolverine is many people's favorite X-Man. He often goes by the name Logan, though his actual name is James Howlett. But to most people he's known as Wolverine, and like the wolverine of the northern wilderness (he hails from Cold Lake, Alberta, in Canada), he's known for his ferocity in combat. His most outstanding mutant power is the ability to heal almost instantly from any wound, even a bullet to the skull.

Wolverine's other most noteworthy features are his adamantium claws. Scientists working for William Stryker performed surgery on Wolverine at a secret facility at Alkali Lake, grafting near-indestructible adamantium to his skeleton, including his bone claws, which are ready to spring from between his knuckles for use as lethal weapons.

Wolverine is said to be a typical antihero due to his brooding nature and willingness to use deadly force—plus he seems to lack traditional heroic qualities such as idealism and morality. He's famous for saying, "I'm the best there is at what I do, but what I do best isn't very nice."[64] But is he really an antihero? He certainly doesn't lack heroic qualities like courage. And despite his rebel nature, when Cyclops complains that there's no way Wolverine is going to take orders, Charles Xavier replied, "Give him an order worth following."[65]

Wolverine bears an uncanny resemblance to the savage Bible hero Jehu. Around 840 BC, the king of Israel was an evil man named Joram, who worshipped the demon-god Baal. One day a prophet of God arrived and anointed his top general, Jehu, as king. God then commanded Jehu to slay Joram, wipe out his entire family, and avenge the blood of His prophets that Jezebel, Joram's mother, had murdered. Jehu was also commanded to completely eradicate Baal-worship from Israel.

Jehu immediately leaped into his chariot and raced for the capitol, Jezreel. A lookout spotted his chariot churning up dust, and shouted to Joram, "The driving is like that of Jehu son of Nimshi—he drives like a madman!" (2 Kings 9:20 HCSB). Joram got in his own chariot and drove out to meet him, and Jehu, drawing his bow, drove an arrow straight through Joram's heart.

Then Jehu arrived in Jezreel, looked up, and saw Jezebel in a palace window with a couple servants behind her. "Throw her down!" he growled, and they obeyed (2 Kings 9:33 NIV). Within days, Jehu had wiped out the entire royal family. He then ordered every priest of Baal to come to an assembly. When they packed into the temple, Jehu ordered them slaughtered.

Jehu was so ruthless and violent that you scarcely know whether to call such a man a hero, but it took someone like him to root evil out of Israel (see 2 Kings 9:1–10:28). God picked the right man for the job. Jehu was a merciless dog of war—a ruthless killer and a man of action. Like Wolverine, what he did best wasn't very nice.

In *X-Men United*, Colonel William Stryker taunts Logan, saying, "People don't change, Wolverine. You were an animal then, and you're an animal now."[66] But this wasn't true. In the first *X-Men* movie, Logan went through an incredible arc of redemptive transformation. At first, he *was* like an animal. He lived for drinking and cage fights, and he loved beating men into submission simply because he could. When Rogue sees the incredibly messy trailer he lived in, she is taken aback at what a slob he is.

When Logan first discovers that Rogue has hidden

herself in his flatbed trailer, he forcibly removes her. Rogue protests, "Where am I supposed to go?" Logan replies, "I don't know." Rogue asks, "You don't know, or you don't care?" Logan cynically answers, "Pick one."[67] He had a change of heart, however, and let her ride in the pickup cab. Logan slowly developed a strong, protective instinct toward her, and when Rogue ran from Xavier's school, Logan gently urged her to return, saying, "C'mon, I'll take care of you."[68]

His sacrificial love for this troubled teen comes to full bloom at the end of the movie. Even though Logan has been warned that he'll die if he maintains contact with her, he chooses to do it anyway so he can transfer his healing power to her. The scene of wounds opening up on his body and blood pouring down in rivulets through his clothing evokes the image of Jesus dying on the Cross. The Bible says, "Greater love has no one than this, than to lay down one's life for his friends" (John 15:13 NKJV).

And in the movie *X-Men Origins: Wolverine*, when Logan leads a group of young mutants to safety and Deadpool blocks the way, Logan sends the group another way while he remains to fight and possibly die. Stryker was wrong. People *do* change. Logan had indeed been an animal, but he transformed—and there is hope that we can all change.

Don't ever give up on yourself, no matter what a failure or self-centered slob you've been. Jesus is in the business of changing lives and His power is adequate for you as well.

MYSTIQUE

20. BLENDING IN

Mystique had one of the most useful mutant powers. In addition to superhuman agility, reflexes, and an accelerated healing factor, she was a shapeshifter who frequently mimicked other people's appearances, manner of dress, and voices. She imitated them so perfectly that few could tell she wasn't the actual person. (About the only clue was that every so often her eyes would glow yellow.) This talent got her into many secure locations and out of many dangerous ones. Although she often presented herself as a beautiful woman, her "default setting" was the appearance of a blue, scaly-skinned mutant with yellow eyes.

As a young girl named Raven, Mystique first met

Charles Xavier—then a boy—when she crept into his parents' mansion looking for food. Charles took her in and she grew up as a member of his family. However, she became discontent with her appearance and always having to hide who she really was. So when a fellow mutant, Hank McCoy, sought a cure to make them both appear normal, Mystique was eager for it.

But Magneto, infatuated with mutant powers, told Mystique that she was perfect as she was, and she was so won over by his "acceptance" that at the end of *X-Men: First Class*, she became his faithful follower. Over time, she became highly skilled in martial arts and developed into a ruthless killer. In *X-Men: The Last Stand*, after many years of serving Magneto, she sacrificially jumps in front of him to protect him from a dart containing a "cure" for mutation. As a result, Mystique loses her powers. Magneto then callously abandons her, saying, "I'm sorry, my dear. You're not one of us anymore."[69]

There were also shapeshifters of sorts in the Bible. When his elder brother Esau was out hunting to supply a meal for their father, Isaac, Jacob disguised himself as Esau, went into his father's tent and tricked Isaac into giving him Esau's blessing. Isaac was blind, so Jacob donned one of Esau's robes so he'd smell like him. And since Esau was hairy, Jacob strapped goatskins to his forearms and the back of his neck. Isaac felt Jacob's arm and was convinced it was Esau (see Genesis 27:1–35). Think of it! Brushing your hand against Esau was like petting a goat.

A man named Laban later pulled a similar stunt. When his younger daughter, Rachel, was preparing to go into her wedding tent, Laban sent in his older daughter, Leah, instead. Since the tent was dark and they spoke only in whispers, Jacob thought he was consummating his marriage with Rachel, only to realize the next morning that he'd slept with Leah (see Genesis 29:21–30). Something very similar nearly happened to Wolverine. In *X-Men: United*, Mystique morphed into Jean Grey (whom Wolverine loved) and went to his tent. But her ruse was discovered before things went too far.

Other people of the Bible *literally* morphed. After His resurrection, Jesus supernaturally changed His appearance so He could have a discussion with His disciples without them recognizing Him: "He appeared in a different form to two of them while they were walking. . .to the country" (Mark 16:12 NASB). The angels of God have this ability also, which is why the Bible says, "Do not neglect to show hospitality to strangers, for by this some have entertained angels without knowing it" (Hebrews 13:2 NASB). But beware, because fallen angels can do this too: "Even Satan disguises himself as an angel of light" (2 Corinthians 11:14 NASB).

We Christians are told, "If it is possible, as far as it depends on you, live at peace with everyone" (Romans 12:18 NIV). This often means finding common interests and points of agreement. Paul presented himself as an example of this when he wrote, "I try to find common ground with everyone, doing everything I can to save some" (1 Corinthians 9:22 NLT).

The danger comes when, in your efforts to find acceptance, you go too far, blending in so well with the crowd and becoming so much like everyone else that you fail to stand for the truth of the Gospel. This is where the term "chameleon Christian" comes from. In the end, such believers often find out that the high price they paid for acceptance by others doesn't pay off. When they finally feel compelled to take a stand for the faith—usually over some blatant moral issue—their fickle friends show *their* true colors and ditch them, saying, "Sorry. You're not one of us anymore."

Peter warns, "You have had enough in the past of the evil things that godless people enjoy—their immorality and lust, their feasting and drunkenness and wild parties, and their terrible worship of idols. Of course, your former friends are surprised when you no longer plunge into the flood of wild and destructive things they do. So they slander you" (1 Peter 4:3–4 NLT).

It's fine to seek points of agreement in order to

bring others to the truth, but only so long as you don't compromise your faith. May God give you the wisdom to know the difference.

NIGHTCRAWLER

21. ESCAPING IN A HEARTBEAT

The movie *X-Men United* opens with a bizarre blue mutant with a pointed tail, covered with strange geometric tattoos, repeatedly vanishing and reappearing in swirling puffs of mist. Nightcrawler, as he is called, easily makes his way past White House security but is shot and wounded before he can stab the president with a knife. Immediately he vanishes. The nation is stunned by this close encounter, and Charles Xavier uses Cerebro (a machine that enhances his psychic powers) to try to track the mutant's erratic movements. Charles quickly realizes that Nightcrawler has the ability to teleport.

Storm and Jean Grey fly the X-Jet to where Nightcrawler has sought refuge inside an abandoned Catholic church and persuade him to come with them. He tells them that his name is Kurt Wagner (aka "The Incredible Nightcrawler"). As they examine his tattoos, they see a circular wound on the back of his neck, made by a needle that injected mind-controlling drugs into his body. As it turns out, renegade army officer William Stryker has drugged Nightcrawler and sent him to kill the president in order to "prove" how dangerous mutants are.

Free of Stryker's influence, Nightcrawler reverts to his humble, charming self, and after he joins forces with the X-Men, his amazing ability repeatedly saves the day. When a missile blasts open the X-Jet and Rogue is sucked out, Nightcrawler teleports to her, grabs her in mid-air, then takes both of them back into the jet. And in the climax of the movie, he teleports Storm inside Cerebro, where she rescues Charles Xavier from a mutant that has been controlling his mind.

All this makes for an impressive fictional story, but is teleportation real? Yes, it is. Men of God sometimes traveled from one place to another instantaneously, although the Bible simply calls it "being caught away." A Christian named Philip was in southern Israel on the Gaza Road, where he baptized an Ethiopian eunuch. Then the Bible states, "Now when they came up out of the water, the Spirit of the Lord caught Philip away, so that the eunuch saw him no more. . . . But Philip was found at Azotus" (Acts 8:39–40 NKJV). Azotus was more than ten miles away!

People also believed that Elijah frequently teleported. When Elijah returned to Israel and met Obadiah, he told him to inform the king of his return. But Obadiah objected, "And now you say, 'Go, tell your master, 'Elijah is here!'" And it shall come to pass, as soon as I am gone from you, that the Spirit of the LORD will carry you to a place I do not know" (1 Kings 18:11–12 NKJV).

Jesus also may have teleported to inside a locked house after His resurrection: "When the doors were shut where the disciples were assembled. . .Jesus came and stood in the midst" (John 20:19 NKJV). Alternately, He may simply have passed through the door. At any rate, teleportation doesn't just belong to the realm of science fiction. God has enabled heroes of faith to do it in times of need.

In the comics, Mystique was Nightcrawler's mother, and she gave birth to him in a small village in Bavaria, Germany. But when the local people saw his blue skin and pointed tail, they thought he was a devil and wanted to destroy him. He was rescued from the mob, however, and ended up in Munich, where he was brought up in the circus. He was accepted and didn't look out of place among the freak shows there.

Here's an amazing fact: Nightcrawler was a devout

Catholic. In the movie, he first quoted the Lord's Prayer when he was troubled, then later quoted Psalm 23. When he asked Storm why she had so much anger, she replied, "Sometimes anger can help you survive." Nightcrawler responded, "So can faith."[70]

Faith sometimes grows in unexpected places. You might be surprised to find that people whom you least expect to have faith, are, in fact, believers.

But why does the ability to teleport have such an enduring appeal for many people? Very likely, it ties in closely to mankind's basic "fight or flight" instinct. When people are faced with a life-threatening crisis or an opponent too big to fight, the desire for flight kicks in. David said in such a situation, "The terrors of death have fallen on me. . .horror has overwhelmed me. I said, 'Oh, that I had the wings of a dove! I would fly away and be at rest. I would flee far away and stay in the desert; I would hurry to my place of shelter'" (Psalm 55:4–8 NIV).

God *has* provided a place of shelter for His children, but it's not far away and you don't need wings or teleporting abilities to get there. God Himself is our safe haven: "The LORD also will be a refuge for the oppressed, a refuge in times of trouble" (Psalm 9:9 NKJV). He is frequently compared to a fortress atop an impregnable rock, and you can be there, in the safety of His presence, in a heartbeat—not by teleporting, but by prayer.

22. THE MARK OF THE BEAST

In *X-Men: The Last Stand*, Worthington Labs announces that it has developed a treatment that suppresses the X-gene that gives mutants their powers. They offer this cure to any mutant who wants it. Some, like Rogue (whose touch is fatal to others) are eager for it, but mutants such as Storm are indignant that people think their condition is a sickness.

Others, such as Magneto, see it as a government plot to eradicate all mutantkind. Magneto goes to an old theater where other mutants are discussing the matter, and the speaker states that the cure is voluntary and that nobody is talking about exterminating them. Magneto counters, "No one ever talks about it. They just do it. And you go on with your lives, ignoring the signs all around you. And then, one day. . .they come for you."[71]

Magneto was always a shrill voice warning of a conspiracy against mutants. In the first *X-Men* movie, when Senator Kelly demands that all mutants be registered with the government, Magneto warns, "Let them pass that law, and they'll have you in chains with a number burned into your forehead!"[72] Many Christians identify with Magneto's comment, since it's hard not to see the similarity between Magneto's words and these words from scripture: "A mark on their right hands or on their foreheads" (Revelation 13:16 NIV).

Magneto also warns, "They will force their 'cure' upon us."[73] Unfortunately, he is right to be concerned about the cure. While freeing mutants from an armored convoy, Mystique is shot with a dart and immediately loses her shape-shifting ability. Magneto notes grimly, "They put the cure in a *gun*."[74] So much for it being voluntary. On the other hand, the guard *was* acting in self-defense and the mutants he was transporting were dangerous criminals.

Christians today who believe that we're now living in the end times constantly watch the news for fulfillments of Bible prophecy. And the Bible does warn of things to come. Instead of being asked to turn themselves in to receive a cure for mutant powers, however, Christians will be pressured to deny their faith in Christ. And the Bible says many will do so. Many are *already* doing so, in fact, and the pressure will become even more intense.

Jesus told His followers, "Then they will deliver you to tribulation, and will kill you, and you will be hated by all nations because of My name. At that time many will fall away and will betray one another and hate one another. . . . Because lawlessness is increased, most people's love will grow cold" (Matthew 24: 9–10, 12 NASB). Also, the apostle John warns that the propaganda minister of the Beast "forced all people. . .to receive a mark on their right hands or on their foreheads, so that they could not buy or sell unless they had the mark" (Revelation 13:16–17 NIV).

The Bible says that those who hold out and refuse to surrender to the world government will be hunted down, just as the Sentinels in *X-Men: Days of Future Past* hunted and exterminated all mutants. That movie gives a chilling apocalyptic vision of the coming days.

Some Christians constantly get stirred up over new technology that allows scientists to implant computer chips under people's skin, but we've had so many false Mark-of-the-Beast alarms over the decades that it's hard to get excited anymore. As Bruce Banner said mockingly, "Ooh, it's definitely the end times."[75] Nevertheless, personal computer chips *are* becoming more of a reality with every passing year. And considering the alarming state of the world, it's possible that totalitarian regimes could rise and enact draconian laws in order to preserve the wealth and power of the global elite. And this will ultimately result in a one-world regime that will demand full control over the masses.

Mystique accused Francis Xavier of wanting to engage with the world instead of fighting it as Magneto did: "No matter how *bad* the world gets, you don't wanna be against it, do you? You want to be part of it."[76] Indeed, in *X-Men 3*, Hank McCoy was the U.S. government's Secretary of Mutant Affairs.

On the other hand, some people consider the world utterly doomed, so much so that they've completely given up on it and retreated from interacting with it. They quote, "Come out from among them and be separate, says the Lord" (2 Corinthians 6:17 NKJV), and retreat to a figurative cabin in the woods. But if you despair that the world is getting so bad that it can't last much longer, you won't invest in an education or career, and you won't put away retirement savings. You might end up staying awake all night, draped in linen sheets, like some of the Millerites in 1844, waiting for the Lord to rapture you.

Jesus said, "Now when these things begin to happen, look up and lift up your heads, because your redemption draws near" (Luke 21:28 NKJV), but He also told a parable in which He advised, "Occupy till I come" (Luke 19:13 KJV). And to do that, you can't believe every conspiracy theory you hear. Solomon once wrote, "Only simpletons believe everything they're told! The prudent carefully consider their steps" (Proverbs 14:15 NLT). To be truly prudent means wisely and correctly interpreting world events unfolding around us daily.

CAPTAIN AMERICA

23. SUPERHEROES OR VIGILANTES?

In the movie *Avengers: Age of Ultron*, the Avengers cause massive damage to a city in the eastern European nation of Slovakia when they attack a Hydra base there. They had been engaged in a heroic effort to destroy an evil organization, but there was, unfortunately, great collateral damage and many civilians perished.

The Avengers had, so they thought, been operating with the necessary authority. Nick Fury, head of SHIELD, had assembled them and given them a mandate to act. But the repercussions of their recent actions called their entire modus operandi into question. In *Captain America: Civil War*, the United Nations reacts by drawing up The Sokovia Accords. General Ross informs Captain America and the other Avengers, "While a great many people see you as a hero, there are some who prefer the word *vigilante*. You've operated with unlimited power and no supervision, and that's something the world can no longer tolerate."[77]

While the issues in that situation were complex, in several recent movies superheroes have indeed administered vigilante justice. While watching a superhero movie, have you ever been struck by the realization that there's no way they would get away with such things in today's world—with literally executing their foes in the name of justice, revenge, or self-defense? Think of Daredevil tracking down criminals and disposing of them in a bar, Wolverine dispatching enemies in public in Japan, or Deadpool gunning down large crowds of enemies on a major highway in an American city.

Where are the police cars showing up to cordon off the murder scene? Where are the warrants for the super-powered protagonists' arrests? Where are the court cases that dominate the news and drag on for years? You may think I'm being a killjoy by asking these questions, and you may secretly protest, "It's *just* a movie! Let them kill a few bad guys!" But the fact is, this is a major plot hole in many superhero movies, and it's very good that *Captain America: Civil War* finally began to address this issue.

In the past, comicbooks and movies avoided this problem by having superheroes deliver defeated villains to the authorities. In the Spider-Man comics, the police often showed up at a crime scene to find a thug waiting for them, bound in webbing. In the movies, when villains like Green Goblin and Dr. Octopus died, it was by accident. Spider-Man even tried to save Dr. Octopus.

But eventually superheroes began to change. In the movie *Batman Begins*, Batman and the villain Ra's al Ghul are battling atop a speeding train. Just before it plunges off the rails and explodes, Batman tells him, "I won't kill you. . .but I don't have to save you."[78] He then leaps to safety, leaving Ghul to perish.

Most fans didn't bat an eye. After all, Ghul was a terrorist who was plotting mass destruction in a major American city, so he "deserved" to die. But that started Batman on a slippery downward slope; a few years later he forged a Kryptonite spear to plunge through Superman's heart. . .merely on the *suspicion* that Superman was a menace to society.

Whatever your feelings about murder in works of fiction, you're probably relieved that you *don't* live in a failed state where revenge killings are acceptable, where "might makes right," and where mob rule threatens basic human rights. As inadequate as our justice system can be at times, we are still a nation of laws. Judges 17:6 (KJV), referring to a turbulent period in Israel's history when there was no strong central government, says, "In those days there was no king in Israel, but every man did that which was right in his own eyes." Judges 21:25 repeats this chilling statement word for word.

We must obey the laws of the land, and we must obey God's moral laws. King David is an excellent example of the attitude we should have. God had anointed David as the new king of Israel, but King Saul—insane with jealousy—began relentlessly hunting him. Saul's hands were soon covered with blood. He ordered the murder of 85 innocent priests whose only "crime" was giving David refuge (1 Samuel 22:9–19).

Many Israelites wished to see Saul meet his end. Yet despite this, David refused to kill Saul, even though he twice had clear opportunities to do so (see 1 Samuel 24, 26). The men who wanted Saul gone said, "This is the day the LORD spoke of when he said to you, 'I will give your enemy into your hands for you to deal with as you wish'" (1 Samuel 24:4 NIV). And how *did* David wish to treat Saul? He said, "Surely the LORD will strike Saul down someday, or he will die of old age or in battle. The LORD forbid that I should kill the one he has anointed!" (1 Samuel 26:10–11 NLT).

There are clear lessons in this for us. We may be tempted to take matters into our own hands, to do what seems right in our own eyes to "even the score" with our opponents, but we do well to look to the Bible for guidance when seeking justice.

SPIDER-MAN

24. THE POWER OF FORGIVENESS

Sam Raimi has spoken disparagingly of his third Spider-Man movie, admitting that he hadn't been enthused about the villain Venom so he didn't depict him with the passion comicbook fans had been expecting. But judging by the number of people who turned out to see this movie, Raimi definitely got some things right. And of all the Spider-Man movies, this one had the clearest spiritual message.

In *Spider-Man 3*, Peter Parker and Mary Jane ride his moped to Central Park. While they are there, a meteorite falls and an alien entity resembling a tar-like substance exits the meteorite and hitches a ride on Peter's moped. It was a Symbiote, a parasite that bonded with people and took over their minds. For it to gain possession, the person had to yield to dark emotions.

This happens to Peter when he hears from the police that his uncle Ben's *actual* killer is a convict named Flint Marko, who had recently escaped prison. Peter thirsts for revenge and this opens the door for the Symbiote to envelope him. Later as Spider-Man, under the Symbiote's influence, he finds his powers enhanced, though he is much more aggressive and selfish.

This change in Peter alienates Mary Jane. To make matters worse, a photographer named Edward Brock is hired to replace him at the *Daily Bugle*. But when Peter discovers that Brock has altered photos of Spider-Man to make him appear like a villain, he confronts him. Brock pleads for mercy, saying this would ruin him, but Peter sneers. "You want forgiveness? Get religion."[79] He then reports Brock to the newspaper, and he is fired.

Peter's Aunt May, a devout Christian, had always been a strong moral influence on him. (She knelt and prayed the Lord's Prayer in the first Spider-Man movie.) When Peter shares his desire for revenge, she says, "It's like a poison. It can take you over. Before you know it, turn us into something ugly."[80]

Peter is undeterred, however. He even decides to get petty revenge on Mary Jane. He takes Gwen Stacy to the nightclub where Mary Jane works, just to make her jealous. When a scene happens at the nightclub, Peter gets in a fight with the bouncers and accidentally hits Mary Jane. He then realizes the change that has come over him. Desperate to be free of the Symbiote, he dons his Spider-Man duds and makes his way to a church bell tower only to find that it is too strong. However, the ringing of the church bells weakens it, and in a scene resembling an exorcism, he is able to rip it from his body and cast it away.

Meanwhile, Brock has gone into the church below, where he gives vent to his hatred. He prays to God, "I come before You, feeling humbled and humiliated, to ask You one thing: I want You to kill Peter Parker."[81] The Symbiote then falls on Brock, transforming him into the villain Venom. Peter tries to warn Brock that although the surge of power initially feels good, he would lose himself to it, and it would eventually destroy him. Peter urges him to let it go, but Brock refuses to listen.

After defeating Venom, Peter goes to see Mary Jane. She convinces him that although they'd hurt each other, they had to forgive. So they reconcile. In fact, Peter has learned his lesson so well that at the end of the movie, when a repentant Flint Marko tells him he is remorseful over killing Uncle Ben, Peter forgives him.

The message behind the story is thoroughly Christian, since love, humility, and forgiveness are at the heart of

Jesus' teaching. The Bible says, "And be ye kind one to another, tenderhearted, forgiving one another, even as God for Christ's sake hath forgiven you" (Ephesians 4:32 KJV).

God knows that it's wrong when someone deliberately offends you, takes advantage of you, gossips about you, or harms you. He understands how these things can hurt you. He also knows that it's a common human reaction to want the other person to feel pain in return.

But only God can administer justice perfectly. So the Bible says, "Do not take revenge, my dear friends. . .for it is written: 'It is mine to avenge; I will repay,' says the Lord" (Romans 12:19 NIV). It takes faith to trust God to make things right and not take matters into your own hands. But He wants you to unhook your fingers from the offense against you and give Him room to work. He wants you to even refrain from praying for vengeance, but instead to forgive the offending party. After all, you have committed offences yourself. God forgives you. . .if you forgive others (see Matthew 6:15).

God is aware when someone maliciously hurts you or callously uses you, and He's not saying that the offense should simply be overlooked. But He asks you to forgive— even though the offending person is guilty. And you should be especially tenderhearted and forgiving toward fellow Christians. You are to live in love, "forgiving one another, if anyone has a complaint against another; even as Christ forgave you, so you also must do" (Colossians 3:13 NKJV).

MR. FANTASTIC

25. WISDOM VERSUS
STRENGTH

In the first *Fantastic Four* movie directed by Tim Story (2005), brilliant physicist Reed Richards calculates that a powerful cloud of cosmic energy is about to sweep past Earth. Convinced that such unique events had triggered periods of accelerated evolution in Earth's past, Reed wants to expose biological samples to the cloud to see what happens. He appeals to his former classmate, Victor von Doom, to send him up to his private research station, and von Doom agrees to do it, in exchange for a majority of the profits from the experiments.

Thus, Reed Richards, Susan Storm, Johnny Storm, Ben Grimm, and Victor von Doom, fly up to the space station, where Ben dons a spacesuit and goes out to place the samples. Only then does Reed learn to his shock that the cosmic cloud will sweep past Earth earlier than anticipated. As a result, they are unprepared and are all, especially Ben, exposed to high doses of radiation. And they all are transformed.

Reed, called Mr. Fantastic, ends up with a power that often gets a little weird. After being exposed to gamma rays, he is able to stretch his body into any shape he wishes. The audience is repeatedly treated to scenes of his body being wound around objects like so much blue gift wrapping.

Reed is a workaholic. Once he begins working on a project, he becomes so narrowly focused that he blocks out everyone. When General Hager asks Reed to track an anomaly—the Silver Surfer—Reed at first refuses because he is about to get married. But then he builds the tracking device on the eve of the wedding, and once it begins sending him signals, he answers his phone in the middle of his marriage vows.

Reed isn't very social. When he remarks about all the strangers at his stag party, Johnny says, "I would have invited some of your friends, but you don't have any."[82] (It was brought out in the comicbooks that Reed was on the autistic spectrum. People with this disorder are characterized by a lack of social skills and difficulties in communication.)

In one scene, when Reed tells Johnny that he needs

to think before he acts, Johnny counters, "Yeah, but you see, that's your problem—you always think, you never act!"[83] And Reed certainly *did* think. He was the brains of the Fantastic Four. To create the kinds of things he was constantly inventing, he would need an exceptional IQ. A number of Marvel superheroes were outstanding geniuses. Besides Reed, there was Hank Pym, Tony Stark, Forge, Herbert Wyndham, Hank McCoy, Bruce Banner, and Francis Xavier. Whenever a new device or machine needed to be invented, one of them would invent it, without fail.

There were very wise men in the Bible as well. King Solomon was called the wisest man who ever lived, but King Uzziah was the most famous inventor: "In Jerusalem he made devices invented for use on the towers and on the corner defenses so that soldiers could shoot arrows and hurl large stones from the walls. His fame spread far and wide" (2 Chronicles 26:15 NIV).

Some Bible geniuses totally missed out on fame. Solomon wrote of such a man: "There was once a small city with only a few people in it. And a powerful king came against it, surrounded it and built huge siege works against it. Now there lived in that city a man poor but wise, and he saved the city by his wisdom. But nobody remembered that poor man. So I said, 'Wisdom is better than strength'" (Ecclesiastes 9:14–16 NIV). In the comicbooks, again and again it was Reed who saved the situation with his wisdom.

It's great to have brains, but it becomes a problem when you depend too much on them, and when you boast about your problem-solving abilities. This is why God says, "Let not the wise boast of their wisdom. . .but let the one who boasts boast about this: that they have the understanding to know me, that I am the LORD" (Jeremiah 9:23–24 NIV). Why is this? Because sometimes no matter how hard you think, the solution eludes you. You often have to get the answer in a bolt of divine revelation.

It *is* good to have knowledge and wisdom. It's certainly better than lacking it. Nevertheless, even extremely smart people are capable of making dumb life decisions. Like Reed, they may be overachievers but neglect their family and social lives. And there are evil geniuses like von Doom, who have a huge mental IQ, but a low emotional IQ. Because they lack empathy, they use their wisdom for evil.

Also, many brilliant people simply ignore God. How smart is *that*? God says of such people, "The wise men are ashamed. . . . Behold, they have rejected the word of the LORD; so what wisdom do they have?" (Jeremiah 8:9 NKJV).

Don't be misled by overconfidence in your intellect. Depend on God first and foremost, for He tells us, "The fear of the LORD is the beginning of wisdom" (Psalm 111:10 NKJV).

INVISIBLE WOMAN

26. THINGS VISIBLE AND INVISIBLE

Susan Storm is known for being able to bend light waves in such a way that she could literally vanish—hence her superhero name Invisible Girl or Invisible Woman. But this isn't her chief power. Her most outstanding ability is mental control over unseen fields of force, which she draws from a theoretical dimension called hyperspace. Sue often generates powerful invisible force fields around herself or other objects and, being nearly indestructible, they protect her or the objects from projectiles, guns, and even lasers.

Storm can manipulate this energy into various shapes, including domes covering a huge area. She can create invisible stairs or floating discs and then walk on them, making it appear as if she's flying. Sue can also push or strike objects with her power, similar to telekinesis. Though in many ways she may not seem like it, she's easily the most powerful member of the Fantastic Four.

Whatever supposed scientific reasons are given to explain how her powers work—such as invisible power fields drawn from hyperspace—a myriad of unseen forces and energies actually *do* exist, and God created them all: "By faith we understand that the worlds were framed by the word of God, so that the things which are seen were not made of things which are visible" (Hebrews 11:3 NKJV). The apostle Paul also wrote, "For by Him all things were created that are in heaven and that are on earth, visible and invisible" (Colossians 1:16 NKJV).

God has given His angels astonishing spiritual powers, and they, like Susan Storm, manipulate spiritual energy to do what we call miracles. One time, Herod Agrippa arrested the apostle Peter and kept him in prison with the intent to execute him. The night before Agrippa did that, Peter was asleep in his jail cell, bound with chains between two soldiers, with guards before the door. Then an angel appeared, woke him, and commanded him to get up quickly. Immediately his chains snapped open and fell off his hands. The angel told him to follow, so Peter did.

Then came the next miracle: "When they were past the first and the second guard posts, they came to the iron gate that leads to the city, which opened to them of its own accord" (Acts 12:10 NKJV; see Acts 12:5–10). The angel never touched the chains or the gate. He apparently just snapped open the chains by projecting invisible power, and then unlocked and swung open the gate with a powerful thrust of spiritual energy. Many Christians believe that when our physical bodies are transformed in the resurrection, we too shall receive such powers, just like the angels (see Psalm 8:4–5; Matthew 22:30; 1 Corinthians 15:42–44).

Susan Storm never showed off her powers. She was, by nature, understated and considerate. She was a mother-figure to her younger brother Johnny after their parents died. Johnny went through a troubled phase when he struggled with alcoholism and engaged in violence, but Susan's concern and steady hand helped him through his difficulties. By the time he was in his mid-twenties, however, he didn't appreciate her continued mothering and protested, "Sue, stop! You're not mom. Don't talk to me like I'm a little boy, okay?"[84]

At first, when Sue's main ability seemed to be turning invisible, her reticent qualities made her nearly invisible in all *other* senses as well. But outward appearances are often deceiving, and Sue had an inner strength that—

like her formidable psionic gifts—came to the fore over time. Reed was the leader of the group, but he was often distant and detached, so it was Sue's maternal influence that kept the Fantastic Four working together. And over time she became more outspoken and was the leader when Reed was absent.

Sue also had a spiritual side. Her brother, Johnny, noted, "Sue had this religious streak she pretty well kept to herself."[85] Many believers are like Sue: withdrawn, unobtrusive, and seemingly not as gifted as others, yet they're often the ones who move mountains through prayer. Like Job, they pray a protective "forcefield" around their homes and families. Job constantly prayed for God's protection and as a result, the devil complained to God, "Have You not made a hedge around him, around his household, and around all that he has on every side?" (Job 1:10 NKJV).

Just as Sue deflected attacks with psionic forcefields, the Lord shields you when you cry out to Him: "The LORD is my strength and my shield; My heart trusted in Him, and I am helped" (Psalm 28:7 NKJV).

Don't worry if you see yourself as weaker and as having less to offer than others. That gives God an opportunity to shine through you. How are you truly strong anyway? The Bible puts it this way: "'Not by might nor by power, but by My Spirit,' says the LORD of hosts" (Zechariah 4:6 NKJV).

Even when you feel weak, you can be strong through the power of prayer. Paul advises, "Be strong in the Lord and in the power of *His* might" (Ephesians 6:10 NKJV, emphasis added). Therefore, "Seek the Lord and *His* strength" (Psalm 105:4 NKJV, emphasis added).

THE TORCH

27. HOT HEADS AND PRIDE

By merely willing it, Johnny Storm could cause his body to burst into flames, hot enough to melt metal, and propel himself through the air at high speed. Small wonder he went by the name "Torch." He would shout, "Flame on!" begin blazing, then turn off his flame and regain his normal body temperature within seconds. He could also hurl fireballs at his opponents and control nearby fires with his thoughts. The plasma field that enveloped and surrounded his body was hot enough to vaporize anything that came his way, including speeding bullets. He could, with some effort, even will himself to go into "supernova" state and burn at 4,000 degrees Kelvin, almost as hot as the sun.

Can people actually be enveloped with fire but not burn? Not normally, but in exceptional cases, yes. When Shadrach, Meshach, and Abednego refused to worship King Nebuchadnezzar's idol, he ordered that a nearby furnace be heated seven times hotter than usual. Then his guards tossed these three men of God into the furnace. They fell into the midst of the inferno, but immediately got up and began walking around. Then Nebuchadnezzar called them and they stepped out. He "saw that the fire had not touched them. Not a hair on their heads was singed, and their clothing was not scorched. They didn't even smell of smoke!" (Daniel 3:27 NLT).

One time, like the Torch, an angel *flew* in the midst of flames: "Then Manoah took a young goat. . .and offered it on a rock as a sacrifice to the LORD. And as Manoah and his wife watched, the LORD did an amazing thing. As the flames from the altar shot up toward the sky, the angel of the LORD ascended in the fire" (Judges 13:19–20 NLT). And as far as battling enemies with flames, or using them to fill people with awe, one famous prophet had power over fire: Elijah called down fire from heaven on three separate occasions (see 1 Kings 18:36–39; 2 Kings 1:9–12).

Johnny Storm was, by nature, hotheaded and rash. At one point, Reed Richards told him, "You need to control yourself, and think before you act."[86] But that simply wasn't

Johnny's style. When a missile was streaking toward the Baxter Building, he had the sudden inspiration to leap over the edge, transform into his flaming alter-ego, and draw the heat-seeking missile away. Guessing what he was about to do, an alarmed Sue cried, "Don't even think about it!" Johnny quipped, "Never do," and hurled himself off the building.[87]

Johnny was convinced that he was "hot" in more ways than one, and in the two earlier *Fantastic Four* movies, he constantly used his good looks and powers to impress women or aggrandize himself. Like Tony Stark, he was a playboy. He was cocky, a showoff, and a blatant capitalist. When Johnny protests that a female army officer, Captain Raye, had been judging him without knowing him, she answered that she actually *did* know him, explaining, "I read your personality profile—confident, reckless, irresponsible, self-obsessed. . .bordering on narcissism."[88] Johnny didn't deny any of it.

Johnny usually gave little thought to faith in God. In the comics, after a being called the Goddess chose Sue but not him, Johnnie was plagued with self-doubt, asking, "Do I really believe in God? I thought I did. . ."[89]

Johnny had only one crash-and-burn moment in the movies—after first encountering the Silver Surfer—but in real life, someone of his rash, egocentric temperament would have set himself up for a fall many times over. The

Bible warns, "Pride goes before destruction, and a haughty spirit before a fall" (Proverbs 16:18 NKJV). And after God humbled the formerly-proud King Nebuchadnezzar, he admitted, "Everything he [God] does is right. . . . And those who walk in pride he is able to humble" (Daniel 4:37 NIV).

You might know somebody who bears a striking resemblance to Johnny Storm, but this is a message we all must take to heart. Each of us has things we're good at, some God-given talent, or some physical attribute that can lead us to think we're pretty hot stuff. Watch out if you do that, because God will see to it that you're humbled. It happened to King Uzziah. For years, God had inspired him with great wisdom, marvelously helped make him great, and made the kingdom of Judah powerful. But human pride made its way into Uzziah's heart, and it led to his undoing: "His fame spread afar, for he was marvelously helped until he was strong. But when he became strong, his heart was so proud that he acted corruptly, and he was unfaithful to the LORD his God" (2 Chronicles 26:15–16 NASB).

Despite Johnny's many flaws, which the movies focused heavily upon, he was bold, self-sacrificial, honest, and—at times—even sensitive. This illustrates how God can forge a hero out of even unlikely personalities. So don't give up on yourself if you have glaring faults such as a hot temper or impetuousness. Ask God to keep you under His control and to help you think before you act. You'll avoid burnout.

THE THING

28. IT'S CLOBBERING TIME

When the Fantastic Four were bombarded with cosmic radiation, Ben Grimm was subjected to much more of it than the others, since he was on a walk outside the space station. Not only was his physical appearance radically altered, but his condition was permanent. He was still six feet tall, but he now weighed 500 pounds. That's because everything from his internal organs to his rocky orange skin was now composed of a stone-like substance.

As one news commentator noted, he looked like some kind of monster or thing. That's where he got his name: the Thing. Ben took this hard, and he constantly complained about how awful he looked and how he wished he could change his appearance. When he broke the news to his fiancée, Debbie, she couldn't handle it. Even after she watched him heroically save many lives, she took off her engagement ring and left it lying on the street.

Ben told a compassionate blind woman, Alicia Masters, "You don't know what it's like out there. Walking around like some kind of circus freak. People staring, whispering..." When she consoled him and told him that being different wasn't always a bad thing, Ben grimly replied, "Trust me, this ain't one of them times."[90]

Although Ben was aware that exposure to a cosmic storm was the direct cause of his metamorphosis, he ultimately blamed God. He said, "If there's a God, He hates me."[91] Ben believed that there *was* a God, however. At one point he looked up to heaven and sarcastically grunted, "Thanks!"[92] He was constantly grumbling and complaining, so much so that he resembled a rocky, orange version of the Jewish father Tevye, from *Fiddler on the Roof*.

In fact, like Tevye, Ben *was* Jewish. This was brought out in a comic titled "Remembrance of Things Past," in which Ben returned to Yancy Street, the New York neighborhood where he'd grown up. Benjamin Grimm is a Jewish name, but though he'd received instruction in the faith, he didn't attend a synagogue but instead ended up leading the Yancy Street Gang. He only avoided a life of crime by being sent away to live with an uncle; from there he joined the Air Force, eventually training as a NASA pilot.

While visiting Yancy Street, Ben fought a supervillain named Powderkeg. Just before being vanquished, Powderkeg wounded an elderly Jewish man, Mr. Sheckerberg. Ben thought the old man was about to expire, so he knelt down and prayed a Hebrew prayer, the *Sh'ma Yisrael*, traditionally recited over the dying. Sheckerberg survived the attack and asked Ben why he hadn't talked about his faith over the years. Ben replied that he didn't want people to think that all Jews were monsters like him.[93]

It always returned to that issue: Ben's preoccupation with his monstrous looks. Beast of the X-Men had similar struggles. He was so disturbed about his physical appearance that he created an antidote to "fix" it—only his antidote didn't work but actually made it worse.

Many people, both past and present, have been depressed about some facet of their physical appearance, and some have asked God why He allowed them to have such a defect. But Paul asks, "Will the thing formed say to him who formed it, 'Why have you made me like this?'" (Romans 9:20 NKJV). In blaming God for allowing him to look like some monstrosity, the Thing was ignoring the fact that his rocky composition also gave him the power to do superhuman feats.

Some Bible superheroes had image issues: "Some brave and experienced warriors from the tribe of Gad also defected to David. . . . They were expert with both shield and spear, as fierce as lions and as swift as deer on the mountains. . . . These warriors from Gad were army commanders. The weakest among them could take on a hundred regular troops, and the strongest could take on a thousand! These were the men who crossed the Jordan River during its seasonal flooding at the beginning of the year and drove out all the people living in the lowlands on both the east and west banks" (1 Chronicles 12:8, 14–15 NLT).

These biblical heroes were almost superhumanly powerful, and they were unstoppable. When people living near the Jordan saw these superheroes crossing the rushing river when it was in flood tide and a mile wide, they didn't try to stop them but just got out of their way. The NLT says they were "as fierce as lions," but the NKJV gives a more literal translation: "whose faces were like the faces of lions." They may not have been easy on the eyes, but they used their great power for good.

Johnny Storm asked about Ben, "He *does* have some kind of rock-like heart, doesn't he?"[94] Indeed he did. In the comics and in the movies, despite his appearance and gruff, grumbling tone, Ben Grimm was courageous, selfless, and loyal. And these inner qualities are, after all, what counts: "Man looks at the outward appearance, but the LORD looks at the heart" (1 Samuel 16:7 NASB).

SILVER SURFER

29. A TENDER CONSCIENCE

Silver Surfer was one of the most powerful foes the Fantastic Four ever fought—and he was merely a forerunner of someone far more potent and dangerous. Galactus was a superhuman entity with the power to create and destroy planets—and he sustained his immense life force by devouring the energy of entire worlds. One day Galactus arrived at the planet Zenn-La, home to an ancient civilization, and was about to destroy it when a man named Norrin Radd offered to lead him to other worlds instead.

Galactus agreed, and he imbued Radd with a portion of his vast power, as well as the ability to absorb the energy of the universe so that he didn't need to eat, drink, or even breathe. Galactus coated Radd with a silver substance that protected him in the frozen vacuum of space, and he gave him a silver surfboard on which to travel to far-flung star systems—and the Silver Surfer came into being. Rarely had a mortal been given such power.

When the Surfer arrived at Earth, he could see that it was full of sentient life and wished to spare it, but he and Galactus had traveled great distances since the last world, and Galactus could wait no longer. Silver Surfer's conscience wouldn't allow him to see Earth destroyed, so he rebelled against his master. In the comicbooks, Galactus eventually turned away but removed much of the Surfer's power and bound him to Earth so he couldn't return to Zenn-La.

The Surfer could use cosmic energy to defend himself and to attack his enemies. One of his most common methods of attack was sending searing bolts of force from his hands. He could also heal living beings, open portals between dimensions, and travel through time.

Though he still had tremendous power, and sometimes used that power to meet his own needs at the expense of others or to gain revenge upon his enemies, his conscience always immediately caused him to repent. In *Silver Surfer* issue 1, he needed money, so he impetuously broke into a bank—because he had the power to do so—and was about to simply take the cash when he caught himself and repented.[95]

In *Silver Surfer* issue 3, he saved a woman's life, only to be fired upon by police who thought he was part of the enemy forces. Their violence so angered the Surfer that he vowed vengeance. Just before launching a powerful attack, he spread out his arms, looked up at the heavens and implored, "Forgive me for what I am about to do! And grant me the *strength* so that I may *forgive* them who have driven me to do it!"[96] To whom was he praying? It clearly looked like he was addressing God.

Another point: although Silver Surfer had determined to seek vengeance but hadn't yet acted, his conscience already bothered him. But he was so angry that he acted anyway. Silver Surfer triggered global cosmic storms that brought all of modern civilization to a standstill. With all electrical systems down, chaos reigned and millions of lives were threatened. Seeing what great harm he was causing, he relented, saying, "I who have sought to *teach*—have instead learned the ways of violence."[97] He had become no better than the ignorant, violent earthlings. He therefore made amends and fixed the problems he had caused.

King David was another man of great power but with a tender heart. Although his anger, lust, and desire for power sometimes motivated him, he always repented. One time, David began to trust in how strong his army was. God had led him, in a series of astonishing victories, to build a mighty kingdom that stretched from Egypt to the Euphrates. But David began to worry about his ability to hold it together, so he decided to count his soldiers. This angered God, and He sent an angel to kill multitudes of Israelites in a plague.

When God opened David's eyes to see the angel standing over Jerusalem with his sword outstretched, David immediately prayed, "Was it not I who ordered the fighting men to be counted? I, the shepherd, have sinned and done wrong. These are but sheep. What have they done? LORD my God, let your hand fall on me and my family, but do not let this plague remain on your people" (1 Chronicles 21:17 NIV). So God stopped the plague.

The prophet Samuel declared about David, "The LORD has sought out a man after his own heart" (1 Samuel 13:14 NIV). David truly loved God, and though he sinned—as he did when he committed adultery with Bathsheba—he also sincerely repented (see Psalm 51).

How do you act when you're given power? Do you rejoice in it and use it to get whatever you want? Do you use it to run roughshod over others? Do you hold yourself accountable to no one, and do you treat others with contempt? God cautions that He will judge the mighty for how they treat the weak and the vulnerable. So be controlled by a tender conscience.

DAREDEVIL

30. SEEING THINGS
DIFFERENTLY

Matt Murdock grew up in Hell's Kitchen, a rough neighborhood of New York City. One day he was accidentally blinded by radioactive material. Though it robbed him of his sight, the radioactivity greatly heightened his other senses, giving him such pronounced sonar abilities that he could "see" via sound vibrations, in much the same way bats "see" with echolocation. Matt's touch became so sensitive that he could read a book simply by passing his fingers over the ink print.

Matt's father, Jack Murdock, was a boxer who raised his son as a single parent. But after the mob killed Jack because he refused to deliberately lose a fight, Matt determined to avenge his death. He learned several kinds of martial arts and launched his career as Daredevil. A *daredevil* is "a reckless person who enjoys doing dangerous things"—and Matt was indeed soon doing dangerous things.

We know from the comicbooks that Matt Murdock was a practicing Catholic and that he had apparently been an altar boy in his youth.[98] One day as Matt sought to solve a mystery, a person named Macabes told him, "You're a somewhat religious man, so I ask that you reach back to the days of your religious instruction. . ."[99] Another entity advised, "Have your Christian friend read his Bible," and stated that Jesus was prophesied to return not as a small, weak child, but as a judge, jury, and executioner—as a lion, not a lamb.[100] All of this resonated with Matt.

Daredevil was known as "the man without fear," which he had to be when tackling villains more powerful than himself. Remember, apart from his acute senses of hearing and touch, he had no superpowers. Anyone can learn martial arts and become a force to be reckoned with, but some men naturally have lightning-quick reactions and superior strength, and these, when combined with courage, transform them into champion fighters and heroes.

Three thousand years ago, another mighty warrior was also a daredevil, a man utterly without fear. His name was Benaiah, and he belonged to an elite group called David's Mighty Men (2 Samuel 23:8, 20). In one battle between Israel and Moab, two of Moab's top fighters—

the Bible calls them "lion-like heroes"—charged out. They were fierce and fast and strong, but when these lion-like heroes challenged Benaiah, down they went.

Benaiah also leaped down into a pit during a snowstorm and killed a *real* lion. How the lion ended up in the pit and why Benaiah jumped in after him, we have no idea. But after a fierce fight, the lion was dead and Benaiah was still standing. Then there was the Egyptian giant—the Bible refers to him as a "spectacular man"—who came at Benaiah with a spear. Holding nothing but a staff, Benaiah snatched Spectacular Man's spear from him and slew him with it. Because of these heroics, David put Benaiah in charge of his personal bodyguard (2 Samuel 23:20–23 NKJV).

Marvel's blind superhero illustrates another important lesson on courage. Paul says, "We walk by faith, not by sight" (2 Corinthians 5:7 KJV). God often asks us to believe that He will provide for us or do a miracle for us, and then has us step out in faith—even when we don't yet see any manifestation of His promise. For example, when ten lepers cried out for Jesus to heal them, He told them to go show themselves to the priests, something people were to do *after* they'd been healed from leprosy in those days. As far as the ten men could see, they still had leprosy, but they believed and obeyed, and "as they went, they were cleansed" (Luke 17:14 KJV).

God probably won't ask you to leap down into a snowy

pit and battle a savage lion, nor will He ask you to fight supervillains blindfolded, depending only on your hearing. But He may ask you to do things that require great faith and courage. When He does that, you can follow this biblical example of faith: "By faith Abraham obeyed when he was called to go out to the place which he would receive as an inheritance. And he went out, not knowing where he was going" (Hebrews 11:8 NKJV).

God will lead you too, even when you can't see the path ahead. He promises, "I will bring the blind by a way they did not know; I will lead them in paths they have not known. I will make darkness light before them, and crooked places straight. These things I will do for them, and not forsake them" (Isaiah 42:16 NKJV). Knowing that God is with you and will never abandon you will keep you from giving in to fear: "The LORD is the one who goes ahead of you; He will be with you. He will not fail you or forsake you" (Deuteronomy 31:8 NASB).

DOCTOR STRANGE

31. THE GREAT POWER OF GOD

Stephen Strange was a brilliant neurosurgeon in New York City whose practice came to an abrupt end when a car accident broke the bones in both his hands. To his chagrin, medical specialists could do nothing, so he began looking for a cure in alternative medicine.

In the comicbooks, Doctor Strange ended up in Tibet, where he met a 500-year-old man named the Ancient One, the world's most powerful sorcerer. In the movie, he traveled to Nepal instead, and the Ancient One was a woman. At any rate, Doctor Strange became a dedicated apprentice, mastering the magical arts before eventually taking the Ancient One's place. He then began a long career of fighting evil sorcerers like Mordo and arch-demons like Mephisto and Satannish.

So what are Christians to make of a superhero who practices sorcery? Is Doctor Strange's power of God? Some people argue that magic is merely a kind of energy that, at present, defies scientific description, but that it is neither good nor evil.

That sounds like the powers of *most* superheroes who draw on unseen energy to fly, teleport, shoot energy bolts, or use telekinesis. What's the difference between Doctor Strange deflecting a bolt of psychic power with a shield of magical force and Invisible Woman deflecting an energy beam with a psionic forcefield? Isn't "magic" simply an unknown power?

In the Bible, angels have God-given power to do miracles. But in Doctor Strange's world, magical power is a little more complex, and it immediately goes sideways. In the movie, the Ancient One explained that they drew energy from other parts of the multiverse to make magic. But as is brought out in the comicbooks, magic comes from potent artifacts and, for the most part, by calling out to powerful other-dimensional entities. Most often, Doctor Strange invokes the names of a union of beings collectively called Vishanti, and named Hoggoth, Oshtur, and Agamotto individually. When he recites his incantations, he's calling upon these beings for their power to perform his spells.

Hoggoth is the most ancient of the Vishanti and is called "the Lord of Hosts;" Oshtur is called "the Omnipotent" and "Lady of the Skies;" and Agamotto is known as "the All-Seeing" and "the Light of Truth." At first glance, this sounds similar to the Christian Trinity. The Bible describes God as all-seeing and omnipotent and calls Him the "Lord of Hosts" more than 250 times. And Jesus said, "I am the light" and "I am. . .the truth" (John 8:12; 14:6 NKJV).

But the parallels end there. The Hebrews called Ishtar, an ancient Near Eastern fertility goddess, Ashteroth, and the similarity between the names Oshtur, Ishtar, and Ashteroth is deliberate. What's more, one of Ashteroth's titles was Queen of Heaven, and Oshtur, ruler of the stars, is called Lady of the Skies.

None of the Vishanti—not even Hoggoth "the Lord of Hosts"—are accurate reflections of the true God. It would be completely wrong to claim that Doctor Strange calling upon the Vishanti for power to perform magic is a picture of Christians receiving a miracle from the triune God. The comicbook writers merely borrowed God's titles and claimed His attributes for these lesser entities. Thus, Doctor Strange's magic isn't simply a manifestation of obscure scientific energy, nor can it be said to come from God.

However, remember that in the Marvel Universe, God

is "the One who is above even gods."[101] Since He created all beings, including Thor and the Norse gods, wouldn't He have also created the Vishanti and given them their power? Yes, He would have. So couldn't we look upon them as archangels having God-given powers, similar to the Valar, the "gods" of Tolkien's Middle Earth? You're certainly free to take this view if you wish. The problem is that it opens the door to the occult, about which the Bible gives serious warnings.

And you should also consider this: in the days of the early Christians, "there was a certain man called Simon, who previously practiced sorcery in the city and astonished the people of Samaria, claiming that he was someone great, to whom they all gave heed, from the least to the greatest, saying, 'This man is the great power of God.' And they heeded him because he had astonished them with his sorceries for a long time" (Acts 8:9–11 NKJV).

Simon practiced the occult, but because the Samaritans believed in God, he cloaked his sorcery in godly terms and claimed that he derived his power from the Almighty. This allowed him to bask in the title, "The Great Power of God." Yet Simon's power came from fallen spirits, and he was "poisoned by bitterness and bound by iniquity" (vs. 23). When Philip came to Samaria preaching Jesus, manifesting the true power of

God, and performing miracles, Simon realized that his sorcery paled in comparison.

So don't be misled by substitutes. *Doctor Strange* is a fascinating film with many eye-pleasing special effects, but it does little to advance the truth about the astonishing God we serve.

WOLVERINE

32. UNDOING PAST MISTAKES

Time travel is frequently used in comics and movies to change the past. While this often comes across like a tired and implausible ploy, it has been done well at times. And sometimes, like it or not, it's necessary, such as when a poorly planned movie mangles a series. This was the case with *X-Men: The Last Stand*. Not only did it diverge widely from the Dark Phoenix Saga in the comics, but in this one movie alone the filmmakers killed off Cyclops and Charles Xavier and had Wolverine brutally murder Jean Grey, the woman he loved.

Where could filmmakers go after this? They had painted themselves into a corner, sending the X-Men franchise into a tailspin. In the years following, Marvel produced several solo Wolverine movies, and also focused on the X-Men adventures decades before Xavier died. They realized that if they were to move ahead, they had to reboot the series, and they did this in the Herculean retcon *X-Men: Days of Future Past*. (A *retcon* is an alteration of previously established facts.)

In this movie, Xavier, Magneto, and a handful of others are the last surviving mutants in a dark future. All others have been eliminated by deadly robots known as Sentinels. However, a mutant named Kitty Pryde has the ability to send a person's consciousness into the past, so she sends Wolverine back to 1973 to stop Mystique from killing Doctor Trask, creator of the Sentinels. Following his death, Mystique had been captured and her DNA used to upgrade the Sentinels, allowing them to adapt to any mutant power.

Wolverine's mind goes back in time, he wakes up in his own body, and then he finds the younger versions of Charles Xavier and Magneto and enlists their help. Together they prevent Mystique from killing Trask, and because she, a known mutant, has saved President Nixon's life, he decides *not* to authorize the anti-mutant Sentinel program. Logan then returns to a changed future where Charles Xavier, Cyclops, and Jean Grey are all alive. If only life were that easy!

Have you ever messed up so badly that you wished you could go back and do it all again—differently? If you're like many people, you probably have. . .more than once. And this is especially true when there is great guilt and pain attached to past events. They can cast a long shadow, and they can haunt you and your loved ones for years. Many suffer broken relationships, tarnished reputations, and seemingly unending ripples of grief over past mistakes and sins.

The bad news first: you can't go back in time and do things over. But here's the good news: despite everything that's happened—your past mistakes and the things others have done to you alike—God's Spirit *can* "make all things new" (Revelation 21:5 NKJV). His deep love and forgiveness can undo the pain and smash the chains that bind you to the past. It doesn't matter how greatly you've sinned, God stands ready to forgive and cleanse: "If we confess our sins, he is faithful and just and will forgive us our sins and purify us from *all* unrighteousness" (1 John 1:9 NIV, emphasis added).

Even Christians have trouble grasping the depth of this promise. But God has also said, "Come now, let us settle the matter. . . . Though your sins are like scarlet, they shall be as white as snow; though they are red as crimson, they shall be like wool" (Isaiah 1:18 NIV). The Hebrew here literally means "though your sins are *double-dyed* in scarlet, permanently stained and not about to fade, they shall become as white as snow."

There was a man in Jesus' day who was possessed by hundreds of demons, so many that they were called Legion (a legion was 5,120 men). The demons made this man a supervillain with astonishing strength: "There met [Jesus] out of the tombs a man. . .who had his dwelling among the tombs; and no one could bind him, not even with chains, because he had often been bound with shackles and chains. And the chains had been pulled apart by him, and the shackles broken in pieces. . . . And always, night and day, he was in the mountains and in the tombs, crying out and cutting himself with stones" (Mark 5:2–5 NKJV). Yet after Jesus cast the demons out of this man, the people found him "sitting and clothed and in his right mind" (Mark 5:15 NKJV), talking with Jesus.

The Son of God can transform the darkest, most hopeless lives. He's done it for countless others and He can do it for you, too. When God forgives your sins, it's as if you'd never sinned. Often, the situation will be completely changed. And even if you have to live with some of the consequences of your past actions, when there's forgiveness, much of the sting is drained out of them.

Allow God's Spirit to wash through you and cleanse you and forgive you. He can do an amazing retcon, purify your wounded spirit, and bring healing to past wounds that otherwise refuse to heal.

ADAM WARLOCK

33. AN IMPERFECT MESSIAH

You may have wondered, "What would it be like if someone produced comicbooks depicting Jesus as a superhero?" Well, Marvel attempted just that. Marvel editor-in-chief Roy Thomas said that the 1970 rock opera *Jesus Christ Superstar* inspired him to create a Messianic superhero. He admitted, "I had some trepidation about the Christ parallels, but I hoped there would be little outcry if I handled it tastefully, since I was not really making any serious statement on religion. . .at least not overtly."[102]

There was an existing Marvel character named "Him," a synthetic, perfect human created by scientists, formed inside a cocoon. He sometimes returned to a cocoon to hibernate, and this cocoon appeared in the Collector's shop in *Guardians of the Galaxy*. In the comics, this hero leads the fight against Thanos, so it is likely destined be a major star in the *Infinity War* movies in 2018 and 2019.

Thomas had Him leave Earth and encounter Herbert Wyndham on a nearby planet. Wyndham is known as the High Evolutionary because he is able to accelerate evolution and has transformed animals into intelligent bipedal beings. Wyndham has also created a copy of Earth. He intends this Counter-Earth as a paradise and has replicated men who are free from evil on it. But one of his earlier creations is wreaking havoc there. Wyndham has transformed a wolf into a super-advanced being called Man-Beast, and this monster goes to Counter-Earth, rules it as a despot, and corrupts the humans with violent traits.

Wyndham therefore gives "Him" the Soul Gem—one of six Infinity Stones—and sends him to defeat Man-Beast. Him is named Adam (the first of his kind), and Wyndham calls him Warlock because, as he says, all men will fear his power. Warlock eventually stopped Man-Beast, but his narcissism leads to him being crucified. However, Warlock then raises himself from the dead. A new religion forms, one that worships Adam Warlock, who then develops a God-complex.

Warlock then travels space, where he encounters an evil being named Magus, a dark version of himself who has been driven insane by overuse of the Soul Gem. After disposing of Magus, Warlock obtains the Infinity Gauntlet with all six Gems and, combined, these transform him into a godlike cosmic being. But the Living Tribunal rules that Warlock can't be trusted with divine power and orders him to divide the Gems among other beings.

By now you may be wishing that Thomas had left well enough alone. Like him, many people were inspired by *Jesus Christ Superstar*. While some songs are deeply moving, some are far from biblically sound. For example, in "Heaven on Their Minds," Judas criticizes Jesus for beginning to believe that He is God, not merely a man. And the song "Superstar" openly questions whether Jesus actually was who His followers claimed He was. Unfortunately, as Paul warned, "If someone comes to you and preaches a Jesus other than the Jesus we preached, or if you receive. . .a different gospel from the one you accepted, you put up with it easily enough" (2 Corinthians 11:4 NIV).

Possibly Thomas had another reason for calling his superhero Warlock. A *warlock* is a male witch or sorcerer, and this is what some Jews who rejected Jesus said He was. In the Talmud, Sanhedrin 43 relates the trial and execution of Jesus, accusing Him of being a sorcerer, and *magus* is an Old Persian word that means a magician or an astrologer. Thomas may not have intended this, but it's striking that *both* names have such a meaning.

Nevertheless, giving Thomas the benefit of the doubt, we can applaud him for attempting to depict the Messiah in comics. And the Warlock series *does* start out as a fascinating allegory. It's not hard to see his parallels: Wyndham sending "Him" to Counter-Earth is like God sending His Son to the world; the Man-Beast represents the Devil; the people he corrupted are a picture of humanity; Adam Warlock is like Jesus; and the religion that worshipped the resurrected Warlock symbolizes Christianity.

However, Thomas's misconceptions about Jesus led him to present a picture of a messiah who fell short of a true Savior, and he offered a warped view of Christ's deity. Jesus wasn't a narcissist with a God-complex. Jesus *was* and *is* God.

The Bible states, "In the beginning was the Word [Jesus], and the Word was with God, and the Word *was* God" (John 1:1 NIV, emphasis added). John later declared, "No one has ever seen God, but the one and only Son, who is himself God. . .has made him known" (John 1:18 NIV). And, unlike what happened to Warlock in the comics, no Tribunal declares Jesus unworthy of exaltation. Paul says, "Being in very nature God. . . . He humbled himself by becoming obedient to death—even death on a cross! Therefore God exalted him to the highest place and gave him the name that is above every name, that at the name of Jesus every knee should bow. . .and every tongue acknowledge that Jesus Christ is Lord" (Philippians 2:6, 8–11 NIV).

IRON MAN

34. OVERWHELMED BY THE WORLD

In his Iron Man outfit, Tony Stark is a force to be reckoned with, but under the titanium alloy armor, he is very human—and unrelenting fear and stress deeply affect flesh-and-blood humans. Plus, living through cataclysms can shake anyone, and Tony Stark is no exception.

In the climax of the movie *The Avengers*, SHIELD concludes that it can't stop the Chitauri invasion, so it launches a nuclear missile at Manhattan, opting to sacrifice the city and the Avengers to save Earth. But Iron Man seizes the missile and guides it through the wormhole toward the Chitauri fleet above. The missile detonates in a tremendous explosion, wiping out the aliens' mothership and paralyzing the Chitauri destroyers and robots on Earth below.

As if the stress from this desperate act isn't enough, Stark's suit then runs out of power, causing him to plummet to Earth. He falls back through the wormhole just before it closes. At the last instant, the Hulk leaps up and catches him.

The movie *Iron Man 3* follows this near-death experience and gives an accurate portrayal of a person suffering from PTSD (post-traumatic stress disorder) and panic attacks. In the trailer to the movie, he says, "I'm Tony Stark. I build neat stuff, got a great girl, occasionally save the world. So why can't I sleep?"[103] For several months, he compulsively creates several dozen duplicates of his updated Iron Man suit in an effort to shut out the fear.

And Tony Stark isn't the only one who suffers after these events; Doctor Erik Selvig is also briefly institutionalized due to the mental trauma he suffered during Loki's attack on Earth.[104]

Many people suffer from post-traumatic stress disorder. While we often hear about members of the armed forces suffering PTSD, it's also common among police officers, ambulance drivers, and those who have been through life-threatening situations, abuse, or severe psychological manipulation. Even ordinary stress, if prolonged, can wreak havoc with a person's mental and emotional health, and millions of Americans endure stress due to financial pressures, family situations, or other unresolved crises.

The apostle Paul knew what this was like. He wrote of his hardships in Ephesus, in the Roman province of Asia, "We are hard-pressed on every side, yet not crushed; we are perplexed, but not in despair" (2 Corinthians 4:8 NKJV). That's when the stress was still manageable. But later things got out of hand, causing him to admit, "We do not want you to be ignorant, brethren, of our trouble which came to us in Asia: that we were burdened *beyond* measure, *above* strength, so that we despaired even of life" (2 Corinthians 1:8 NKJV, emphasis added).

What's the solution for this kind of stress? David declared, "From the ends of the earth, I cry to you for help when my heart is overwhelmed" (Psalm 61:2 NLT). God will hear and answer you, but you will still be required to withstand the pressures and fight.

One time, David and his men went off to war and left their wives and children in Ziklag. In their absence, Amalekite raiders attacked. When David's men returned to the town, "there it was, burned with fire; and their wives, their sons, and their daughters had been taken captive. Then David and the people who were with him lifted up their voices and wept, until they had no more power to weep" (1 Samuel 30:3–4 NKJV). But instead of allowing himself to be overwhelmed, "David strengthened himself in the LORD his God" (vs. 6).

David asked God, "Shall I pursue this troop? Shall I overtake them?" and the Lord answered, "Pursue, for you shall surely overtake them and without fail recover all" (vs. 8). So David and his men tracked the raiders. When they arrived at the Amalekite camp, David's men fought fiercely and routed the Amalekites and, "nothing of theirs was lacking. . .David recovered all" (vs. 19). What an answer to prayer!

Sometimes you'll suffer disaster and feel overwhelmed. Perhaps you have sinned and failed God, and now the devil is trying to convince you that God is obliged to punish you—so you should just call it quits and not bother praying. Instead, do like David did: "David strengthened himself in the LORD," reminding himself that God loved him and could do the impossible in desperate situations. Once he was assured of that, David was encouraged to pray.

Refuse to give up. Turn to God in prayer. You may feel like the situation is hopeless, but during similarly dark times, Nehemiah admonished his people, "Remember the *Lord*, great and awesome, and *fight* for your brethren, your sons, your daughters, your wives, and your houses" (Nehemiah 4:14 NKJV, emphasis added).

But know this: it may not be a quick, easy battle, so you'll first of all need to "strengthen yourself in the LORD."

You do this by reading His Word and praying passionately. King Asa prayed, "LORD, there is no one besides You to help in the battle between the powerful and those who have no strength; so help us, O LORD our God, for we trust in You" (2 Chronicles 14:11 NASB). God will come through for you.

35. WINNERS AND LOSERS

Gambit is a mutant with the unique ability to convert the energy inside inanimate objects into kinetic energy, charging that item so much that it explodes when it strikes something or someone. Gambit prefers small objects like his trademark playing cards, since it takes very little time to charge them and they're easy for him to hurl accurately. Plus, even a single card explodes with the destructive force of a grenade. Gambit can also charge his metal staff with enough energy to bring down a building. In the movie *X-Men Origins*, he battles Wolverine, demonstrating his superhuman speed, fighting style, and acrobatics.

Gambit's names are also charged with meaning. A

gambit is an opening move in chess in which a player risks one or more pawns or some other minor piece to set the stage for a win. In other words, a gambit is a bold gamble. This describes Gambit's proclivity for gambling and his willingness to take calculated risks. His actual name is Remy LeBeau, and *Le Beau* is French for "the handsome one." A beau is also an expression for a rich, fashionable young man. All these things describe him well.

Gambit was born in the Cajun region of Louisiana, and he's proud of his heritage and accent. He is a professional thief and pickpocket, and though he's one of the "good guys" (in the comicbooks he joined the X-Men), his fellow team members don't always trust him.

With his good looks and wild, carefree attitude, Gambit is a natural lady's man. He possesses an intense, hypnotic charm that allows him to persuade others to agree with him and believe what he says.

Most people have a low opinion of smooth-talking, irresistible n'er-do-wells who prey on women, and Paul wrote about such people in 2 Timothy 3:6. But Gambit proved that he wasn't simply a user. He had a deep and sincere love for Rogue, even though her perilous mutant power meant that they could scarcely touch one another.

Some people think Gambit's personality is summed

up in his opening words with Wolverine in *X-Men Origins*. Wolverine asks, "Are you Remy LeBeau?" to which Gambit replies, "Do I owe you money?" When Wolverine tells him, "No," Gambit admits, "Then Remy LeBeau I am."[105] But this is mainly a humorous touch. The quote that *best* sums up Gambit's outlook is the following: "See, the only difference between a winner and a loser is character. Every man has. . .a price to pay. Yeah, I've paid mine in spades."[106]

This is true. In card games, you go through both runs of good fortune *and* misfortune. In life, such setbacks include poor health, financial reversals, or betrayal. Some people go under during hard times, lamenting that life isn't fair and bemoaning the fact that they were ever born. Others, however, refuse to surrender, and they persevere. We all suffer hardships, but your character determines how you respond to adversity and ultimately decides whether you win or lose.

You can even lose it all, like Job did, and suffer prolonged and unwarranted ruin, but if you continue trusting God, you'll come out the other side stronger and more blessed. Many, like Job's wife, may advise you to simply "Curse God and die" (Job 2:9 NKJV). In other words, give up on God and turn your back on Him when it seems that He's turned His back on you. Then, believing God has abandoned you, you'll feel like simply lying down and dying. That's one option. The other is to declare, like Job, "Shall we indeed accept good from God, and shall we not accept adversity?" (vs. 10).

In Colossians 3:12, Paul advises believers to cultivate virtues like mercy, kindness, humility, and longsuffering. The problem with longsuffering, however, is that to acquire it, you usually have to endure long periods of suffering or adversity. As Paul explains elsewhere, "suffering produces perseverance" (Romans 5:3 NIV). But the pain is worth it. Patience and perseverance are tremendous sources of strength that help you overcome: "Take the prophets. . .as an example of suffering and patience. Indeed we count them blessed who endure. You have heard of the perseverance of Job and seen the end intended by the Lord—that the Lord is very compassionate and merciful" (James 5:10–11 NKJV).

Gambit concludes, "If I learnt anything about life, it's this: always play the hand you're dealt."[107] In cards, you'll sometimes get a poor hand. It comes with the territory, and you can't just declare a misdeal and demand another hand. Yet so often in life, we complain about the hand we've been dealt, the genes we've inherited, and the circumstances we find ourselves in, and we then insist that God immediately resolve our problems. But life doesn't work that way. You must learn to make the best of your circumstances, even if you think you're playing a losing hand. Play it right and you'll actually be a winner. As Gambit noted, "the only difference between a winner and a loser is character."

BLACK PANTHER

36. RISING TO THE OCCASION

The Black Panther is not only the name of a powerful superhero, but is the title given to every chief of the Panther Tribe in the fictional nation of Wakanda. This small country is nestled in northeastern Africa, and the present Panther, T'Challa, like the rulers before him, has resisted every one of the Western powers' attempts to colonize the nation, making Wakanda an isolated Shangri-La.

The Black Panther has super-sharp senses and tremendous strength, stamina, speed, reflexes, and agility. Fans are treated to a display of his awesome fighting abilities in *Captain America: Civil War*, in which he matches Captain America blow for blow and tackles powerful foes such as the Winter Soldier. He also wears body armor made from vibranium, rendering him bulletproof, and his vibranium claws are capable of shredding almost anything—even leaving claw marks on Captain America's shield.

A myth states that the Black Panther's unique link to the panther god grants him these powers. Actually, his power resides in the fact that, as chief, he has the right to eat the mysterious heart-shaped plant, and its potent juice and phytonutrients transform him into a superhero.

Some 10,000 years ago, a meteorite struck Wakanda, leaving a deposit of vibranium, a rare (fictional) element that absorbs sound and vibrations. It also emits radiation that, in the early days, mutated several Wakandans into tormented beings. So Bashenga, the first Black Panther, created a cult to the Panther god to guard the mound and keep people away. Over the millennia, Wakanda's vegetation absorbed the radiation. This includes the heart-shaped herb, and the unique genetic properties of the herb then bestowed beneficial powers.

The myths surrounding the Wakandan meteorite are similar to a myth from the ancient Roman city of Ephesus. When the city rioted against Paul for insisting "that gods made with hands are no gods at all," the city clerk protested, "What man is there after all who does not know that the city of the Ephesians is guardian of the temple of the great Artemis [Diana] and of the image which fell down from heaven?" (Acts 19:26, 35 NASB). This "image" was a large meteorite, and, according to the historian Pliny, it was displayed above the entrance of the temple.

In the comicbooks, during the last century Wakanda began discreetly selling vibranium to outside nations. This brought wealth and a highly educated class, so Wakanda rapidly became an advanced society. Their chief enemy was a man named Ulysses Klaue, who constantly tried to steal vibranium. In the movie *Avengers: The Age of Ultron*, Ultron seizes some vibranium from Klaue at a South African shipyard.

In *Captain America: Civil War*, King T'Chaka of Wakanda is speaking at a UN gathering in Vienna, Austria, when a terrorist bomb kills him. A surveillance camera reveals that the Winter Soldier is responsible, so T'Chaka's son T'Challa sets out after him. Even though T'Challa is now king of Wakanda, he doesn't hesitate to plunge into the thick of battle to right a wrong.

Some 3,000 years ago, David, too, was both king and warrior. Even though he ruled all of Israel, he frequently led his armies into battle.

David was one of Israel's mightiest fighters. Once, before he ascended the throne, he led a small patrol west of Socoh, looking for Philistines. David's men were making their way through a barley field near Pas Dammim when they ran into a company of Philistines. A "company" is 100 men, and while we don't know how many men were with David, we know that they became alarmed when, with a shout, the Philistines charged. David's patrol fled, and only David and a warrior named Eleazar remained. They began hacking their way through foes. The battle went on and on . . .and on. When the fighting finally stopped, only David and Eleazar were left standing, and there was a large heap of dead Philistines lying in the field (see 2 Samuel 23:9–10; 1 Chronicles 11:12–14).

Down through the years, David often descended from his throne, put on his battle armor, and rushed into the fighting. This continued until he was old, when his men finally restrained him. Once David led his army to fight the Philistines, and a fierce Philistine giant named Ishbi-Benob attacked him and tried to kill him. Fortunately, an Israelite warrior rescued the king. Then David's men told him, "Never again will you go out with us to battle, so that the lamp of Israel will not be extinguished" (2 Samuel 21:17 NIV).

You may not be the ruler of a fabulously wealthy African nation or the king of Israel, and you may not have superhuman powers, but you too can rise to the occasion in times of need.

While being a superhero may seem glamorous, it's

often basically little more than being a glorified street fighter. It wasn't beneath David and T'Challa to leave their thrones, doff their royal robes, and fight hard for a worthy cause. Are you willing to be a hero and do what needs to be done?

STAR-LORD

37. RESPECT FOR DIVINE POWER

The amazing thing about the film *Guardians of the Galaxy* is that even though it's often comedic and flippant in tone, it deals with a very serious subject—the destruction of the Nova Empire's capital world, Xandar—and draws heavily upon the lore of the six Infinity Stones. Without this movie, our understanding of the Marvel cinematic universe would be incomplete.

As a child, Peter Quill was abducted from Earth by aliens. As an adult, Quill works with an extraterrestrial named Yondu as a space pirate. Quill (calling himself Star-Lord) goes to the desolate planet Morag, where he steals a mysterious Orb from a temple. Yondu wants them to sell it, but Quill betrays him, intending to sell it on his own. He has no idea, however, how deadly or valuable it is.

Sometime later, he asks, "This Orb has a real shiny blue. . .Ark of the Covenant, Maltese Falcon sort of vibe. What is it?"[108] As he would later learn, the comparison to the Ark of the Covenant was very fitting, for the Orb is the outer casing for the Power Stone, one of six immensely potent Infinity Gems.

An alien named Ronan also wants the Orb, intending to trade it to Thanos, who'd use it to destroy the planet Xandar. Thanos is one of a few entities who could handle an Infinity Stone, because he was an Eternal; the Stone annihilates lesser beings. So Ronan sends Gamora (Thanos's adopted daughter) to get the stone from Quill. But two bounty-hunters—Rocket Raccoon and Groot—are soon chasing Quill as well. The four of them get into a fight, for which they are arrested and sent to prison. Together with Drax the Destroyer, they join forces to become the Guardians of the Galaxy and escape prison.

As the movie unfolds, Quill betrays Yondu again; Gamora betrays Ronan and Thanos; Drax betrays them all to Ronan; and Ronan betrays Thanos. Meanwhile, the Guardians take the Orb to the Collector, only to have his assistant try to steal it. . .but the Stone destroys her and much of the Collector's shop. Peter and Gamora then realize how dangerous the Stone is, and they decide to hand it over to Nova Headquarters.

However, Ronan arrives and seizes the Power Gem. He is about to annihilate Xandar when Quill distracts him then steals it back. As it begins destroying Quill, the other Guardians join hands with him. Together they contain its power and, as a result, Xandar is spared.

Humans are frequently irreverent toward God, and this, combined with their ignorance of His immense power, often results in catastrophe. In the days of the Judges, the Israelites were locked in combat with the Philistines. The Philistines had superior iron weapons, so the Israelites decided to bring the Ark of the Covenant to the battlefront. The Ark was a gold-covered chest, symbolizing the presence of the most holy God, but the Israelites treated it as a giant good luck charm.

The Philistines not only defeated the Israelites, but they also captured the Ark itself. Gleeful, they carried it to Ashdod and set it at the feet of their idol Dagon, believing that he had given them victory over the Israelites' God. But Dagon's idol fell down broken before the Ark. Then a deadly plague broke out in the city, killing many Philistines. Terrified, they sent the Ark to Gath, but plague broke out there also, so they sent it to Ekron. But the Philistines of Ekron wailed, "They have brought the ark of the god of Israel around to us to kill us" (1 Samuel 5:10 NIV).

The Philistines finally learned respect for the power of

God, so they returned the Ark to Israel, and soon it arrived by ox-cart in Beth-Shemesh. The Israelites were overjoyed to see it, but like the Philistines, they, too, suffered for their irreverence: "God struck down some of the inhabitants of Beth Shemesh, putting seventy of them to death because they looked into the ark of the LORD" (1 Samuel 6:19 NIV).

Too often people today are also irreverent toward God, treating Him more like an abstract concept than an Almighty Being. This is because they're ignorant of His holiness and power. They're merely curious about Him, wanting to lift the lid of the Ark and peek in and see if there's anything to this "God" thing. Others have already decided that there's nothing to fear, and smugly set Him down before their idols of rationalism and naturalism, believing that man's wisdom has triumphed over such superstitions.

We are to be in awe of God and respect Him, because just when we finally whittle our concept of God down to size and think we've explained away all the miracles in the Bible and rationalized all His doings, He demonstrates His power and bursts out of the narrow confines we've tried to stuff Him into, leaving us with our fingers burned.

DEADPOOL

38. SUPER BUT NO HERO

Wade Wilson (Deadpool) was a supervillain when he originally showed up in the comic series *The New Mutants* and in the series *X-Force*, and he was downright evil when he made his ominous entrance in the movie *X-Men Origins: Wolverine*. By the time his origin story was rebooted in the 2016 movie *Deadpool*, however, he had evolved into a complex character depicted in varying shades of grey, some very dark.

When a friend calls Deadpool a superhero, he replies, "I may be super, but I'm no hero."[109] This admission captures the heart of the movie. But if he's not a superhero, what *is* he? He's no longer a supervillain. And you can truly empathize with his humanity when he's handed the news that he has an aggressive form of cancer in several organs. Then a recruiter approaches him with a radical new treatment and promises, "We can give you abilities most men can only dream of. . . ."[110]

But things only became more tragic. Desperate for a cure, Wade subjects himself to literal torture to trigger a life-saving mutation. But though he receives powers—superhuman agility and an ability to heal at an accelerated rate—he is badly disfigured and mentally unstable.

Much of the appeal of this movie is that it "breaks the fourth wall" by having the protagonist acknowledge to the audience that he's a fictional comicbook character. And many people are amused by his nonstop self-referential humor and get laughs out of the constant foul language and sexual jokes. Like an adolescent with a motor-mouth, Deadpool seems unable to take things seriously. It brings to mind what Steve Rogers asked Tony Stark, "Is everything a joke to you?"[111]

Wade is also often very crude, and this, too, would have drawn comments from Captain America. Not only does Cap chide, "Language!" when Iron Man utters a profanity,[112] but he's also famous for asking, "What's the deal with all that potty-mouth stuff, huh? Why does every movie these days have to feel like a sailor wrote the script?"[113]

It's no secret that Captain America is a Christian, or that his views are profoundly shaped by the New Testament, which states, "Obscene stories, foolish talk, and coarse jokes—these are not for you. Instead, let there be thankfulness to God" (Ephesians 5:4 NLT).

Deadpool also strikes many peoples' funny bones with the way he gleefully guns down people in the streets, taking a perverse delight in killing. And when Colossus is in the middle of giving a rousing speech on being a superhero and doing good, Deadpool ignores him. Immediately after Colossus praises showing mercy to one's enemies, Deadpool puts a bullet through Ajax's brain. Obviously, he considers all the traditional superhero virtues a joke.

Deadpool is reminiscent of King Saul in the Bible, a great warrior who, later in life, became mentally unstable. Saul had been an unstoppable man of war: "He fought against his enemies in every direction—against Moab, Ammon, Edom, the kings of Zobah, and the Philistines. And wherever he turned, he was victorious. He performed great deeds and conquered the Amalekites, saving Israel from all those who had plundered them" (1 Samuel 14:47–48 NLT). But after he'd disobeyed God for years, the Lord removed the protection of His Spirit, leaving Saul open to attacks of the devil. The Bible tells us, "The Spirit of the LORD had left Saul, and the LORD sent a tormenting spirit that filled him with depression and fear" (1 Samuel 16:14 NLT).

And Saul, like Deadpool, had a foul mouth. When Saul's son Jonathan stood up for David, "Saul boiled with rage at Jonathan. 'You stupid son of a whore!' he swore at him" (1 Samuel 20:30 NLT). The footnote to the Living Bible candidly informs us, "The modern equivalent is 'son of a bitch.'" Given the dark place Saul's mind was in, you can be sure that he had a very foul mouth much of the time.

Many modern Christians seem to think that bad language is a non-issue—that it's even a virtue that they proudly cling to make it clear that they're relevant in today's world and not self-righteous or overly religious. But they're invariably able to bite their tongue and keep their speech clean when they're in "polite" company—which goes to show that they can control it. This demonstrates that it's a conscious choice to use foul language.

Much of Deadpool's appeal stems from the fact that his outlook and lifestyle resonate with people in today's world. As he confessed, he had super powers, but he was no hero. He makes no pretense at being a hero, of holding himself to a higher moral code, or of emulating Christ—and since he's not a believer, we shouldn't expect him to. But since this attitude describes so many people today, they applaud him as someone to identify with.

As Christians, we should avoid coming across as self-righteous, but the fact remains that we are to follow in the footsteps of Christ and emulate His attitudes and actions—and this will definitely make us different from most people in the world.

ELEKTRA

39. SEEKING REVENGE

Elektra Natchios was the daughter of Nikolas Natchios, a wealthy Greek businessman. Her father's riches allowed her to pursue a career in the martial arts of China, Japan, and Southeast Asia, and she wielded a pair of bladed Okinawan sai as her trademark weapons. In the comicbooks and in the movie *Elektra*, she hires herself out as an assassin. Since Matthew Murdock is an idealistic lawyer defending the poor by day and a superhero defending the weak by night, it might seem surprising that they become romantically involved.

Elektra's origin story in the movie *Daredevil* (2003) explains how she came to walk such a troubled path. She wasn't originally an assassin but simply a privileged young woman who happened to be proficient in deadly fighting skills. Matt had also mastered several martial arts, and in the movie, shortly after meeting her, he battles Elektra to a draw in a children's playground. Yet it is more a savage mating dance than actual combat, as they soon fall in love.

The problem arises with Elektra's father, Nikolas. He had dealings with Wilson Fisk—a crime boss known as the Kingpin—and when Nikolas attempts to end his relationship with the mobster, Fisk hires a hit man named Bullseye to eliminate him. Matt attempts to stop the assassin, but Bullseye catches one of Daredevil's fighting sticks (his disassembled cane), and hurls it at Nikolas with lethal force, impaling him. This tricks Elektra into believing that Daredevil has killed Nikolas.

Overcome with grief, Elektra vows vengeance on Daredevil. She finds him, wounds him with her sai, then removes his mask to look upon his face. She is stunned to learn that it is the man she loves, and only too late does she realize that Matt is innocent. Elektra is then forced to fight Bullseye alone, and she dies at his hands. She is later resurrected, and in the movie *Elektra*, she has become an assassin. She gains redemption, however, when she refuses to assassinate someone she'd been contracted to kill.

Because you often don't have all the facts, you're apt to misjudge and strike out in anger against the innocent. This is one of many reasons the Bible forbids seeking revenge. Also, the "justice" you mete out might far exceed the offense.

Matt Murdock also struggles with the fine line between justice and vengeance. He was a practicing Catholic, and when he goes to confession, he tells Father Everett, "Justice isn't a sin, Father." But the priest replies, "No, but vengeance is. . . . Is that how you want to live your life? A lawyer during the day, and then judge and jury at night?"[114]

You probably won't seek vengeance with a pair of sai—at least we can hope not—but you will be tempted at times to get back at those who offend you. You want to get even, to make others hurt like you've been hurt. You know it's wrong, but it can give a sense of pleasure to know you've caused others pain. It can feel so "right" that it can be difficult to believe it's actually wrong. But the Bible warns, "Do not say, 'I'll do to them as they have done to me; I'll pay them back for what they did'" (Proverbs 24:29 NIV).

In the Bible, Abner, general of the army of Israel, was fleeing back to his own country after a disastrous battle but was being pursued by Asahel, the brother of Joab, general of the army of Judah. Abner tried to dissuade Asahel from following him, saying, "Stop chasing me! Why should I strike you down? How could I look your brother Joab in the face?" (2 Samuel 2:22 NIV). But Asahel continued his pursuit. So just as Asahel was about to catch him, Abner thrust the butt of his spear through him, killing him with one blow.

All Joab knew or cared about was that Abner had slain his brother, and he was bent on revenge. So some time later, when Abner visited David to make peace between their armies, Joab took Abner aside, pretending that he wanted to speak with him, then murdered him with a sword (2 Samuel 3:12–39). Joab felt justified in his action, but David lamented Abner's death and the circumstances of it. Years later, as David lay dying, he instructed Solomon to kill Joab, and the murder of Abner was the prime reason David sanctioned Joab's death.

Seeking revenge usually starts with bearing a grudge against someone and refusing to forgive them. The more you think about your grudge, the more indignant you become, and the more you desire to strike out against the person who has offended you. The Bible urges us to pursue love, not vengeance, and love keeps no record of wrongs. So, "Do not seek revenge or bear a grudge against anyone among your people, but love your neighbor as yourself" (Leviticus 19:18 NIV).

40. ATTITUDES AND PRAYER

In the comics, after being warned that a deadly foe was about to attack him because of his affinity to spiders, Peter Parker (Spider-Man) prayed. He may not have had all his doctrine straight, but at least he prayed, saying, "Hey, God? It's Peter again. Listen, not that I'm complaining or anything, but next incarnation. . . you think you could have me get bitten by a radioactive Jennifer Lopez?"[115]

Peter was giving credence to reincarnation, which is at odds with the Bible's teachings. Such syncretism of religious beliefs is common today. The spiritual views in comicbooks usually reflect the beliefs of the world, not actual Christian teaching.

But even though most comicbooks have truth mixed with folklore, you shouldn't automatically write them off. We're to engage people where they're at, just as Jesus did with the Samaritan woman. The Samaritans were descended from pagans who had intermarried with Israelites centuries earlier, and they mixed their own beliefs with Hebrew monotheism (2 Kings 17:27–34). By Jesus' day, the Samaritans worshipped only the Lord, even though, as Jesus told the woman, "You Samaritans know very little about the one you worship" (John 4:22 NLT).

But instead of insisting that the woman worship God at the designated Jewish place of worship, Jerusalem, and in the Jewish way—following all the religious laws and rules—to be in right standing, Jesus told her that God now accepted anyone who worshiped Him "in spirit and in truth" (vs. 23).

Paul told the Greeks of Athens, "As I was passing through and considering the objects of your worship, I even found an altar with this inscription: TO THE UNKNOWN GOD. Therefore, the One whom you worship without knowing, Him I proclaim to you: 'God, who made the world and everything in it. . . . Gives to all life, breath, and all things. . . . So that they should seek the Lord, in the hope that they might grope for Him and find Him" (Acts 17:23–25, 27 NKJV).

Peter Parker was one such person groping through life, trying to find the Lord. In the comicbooks, he often had spontaneous conversations with God, usually consisting of complaints and questions about things He had allowed to happen to him or to his loved ones. But Peter also prayed prayers of gratitude. He and Mary Jane Watson had married and, for the most part, had a good relationship. But at one point, there was great strain upon their marriage. One night, as Peter lay awake contemplating Mary Jane beside him, he felt extremely grateful, and prayed, "So here's the thing, God. . .I know I complain a lot, and I know that you and me, we've got issues, but right now, just for tonight. . .Thank you for her. Thank you."[116]

Depending on where you're at in your walk with God, you'll identify more either with Peter's prayers of complaint or his prayers of thankfulness. The Bible says, "I will bless the LORD at all times: his praise shall continually be in my mouth" (Psalm 34:1 KJV) and "let us offer the sacrifice of praise to God continually. . .our lips giving thanks to his name" (Hebrews 13:15 KJV). Yes, we are to bless the Lord "at *all* times," even when things are going wrong. But that's a tall order for most people.

It's easy to feel grateful when things are going your way, when all your needs are met, when you have no major health issues, and when you're not suffering a crisis. But just see what happens when you're under pressure. Even Job, the most spiritually mature man on Earth in his day (Job 1:8), after months of unrelenting suffering (7:3), filled chapter after chapter with his protests to God. He protested, "My complaint is bitter. . . . Oh, that I knew where I might find Him, that I might come to His seat! I would present my case before Him, and fill my mouth with arguments" (23:2–4 NKJV).

There are often two stages in our relationship with God. The Bible says of the first stage, "Anyone who comes to him must believe that he exists *and* that he rewards those who earnestly seek him" (Hebrews 11:6 NIV, emphasis added). Peter Parker often exemplified the first stage. He believed that God existed, which is why he talked to Him—but from his limited experience, he didn't think God was usually willing to change his circumstances. So he complained and questioned.

Those living in the second stage not only believe that God exists, but they also trust that He will eventually reward them by answering them if they earnestly seek Him and don't give up. David admitted, "I had fainted, unless I had believed to see the goodness of the LORD in the land of the living" (Psalm 27:13 KJV).

If you believe God will eventually respond to you, you can maintain hope and a positive attitude. Even if you don't necessarily believe that God will give you all your rewards in this life, if you believe that He will abundantly bless you and make things right in eternity, you can have joy and more easily accept the rough-and-tumble of this world.

PROFESSOR X

41. BEWARE WHAT YOU THINK

Mutants like Charles Xavier, Jean Grey, and Emma Frost were able to read other people's thoughts. In the 2000 movie *X-Men*, when Cyclops asks Charles Xavier how he knew that he (Cyclops) didn't like Wolverine, Xavier replies jokingly, "Well, I am psychic, you know."[117] But Xavier's mind-reading abilities weren't switched on 24/7. For example, he'd promised Raven (Mystique) that he would never read her mind, so he obviously had control over his powers and could decide when to focus on someone and listen in and when not to. In the beginning, when they are on friendly terms, he requests permission to access Magneto's memories before actually doing so.[118]

You may wonder: Are such gifts real outside the movies? Yes, they are. For starters, God knows absolutely everything and knows what every person on Earth is thinking at any given moment. David wrote, "You understand my thought from afar. . . . Search me, O God, and know my heart; try me and know my anxious thoughts; and see if there be any hurtful way in me" (Psalm 139:2, 23–24 NASB). And David advised Solomon to worship and serve God, "for the LORD sees every heart and knows every plan and thought" (1 Chronicles 28:9 NLT).

Jesus is the most outstanding example in the Bible of someone who had the ability to read minds. When a sick man's friends brought him to Jesus for healing, "he said to the paralyzed man, 'Son, your sins are forgiven.' Now some teachers of the law were sitting there, thinking to themselves, 'Why does this fellow talk like that? He's blaspheming! Who can forgive sins but God alone?' Immediately Jesus knew in his spirit that this was what they were thinking in their hearts, and he said to them, 'Why are you thinking these things?'" (Mark 2:5–8 NIV).

This ability to see into people's hearts gave Jesus a supernatural edge in avoiding danger. John tells us, "Jesus would not entrust himself to them, for he knew all people. He did not need any testimony about mankind, for he knew what was in each person" (John 2:24–25

NIV). This doesn't mean that He heard a full, running dialogue of the thoughts of every person He encountered, but it *does* mean that at a glance He could tell where anyone was at.

As the eternal Son of God, pre-existent in heaven, Jesus was omniscient. But before coming to Earth, "Christ Jesus, who, although He existed in the form of God. . . emptied Himself. . ." (Philippians 2:5–7 NASB). To become a limited human being, Jesus divested Himself of His omnipotence, omnipresence, and omniscience. But often the Spirit gave Him insight. For example, once Jesus saw His disciples in trouble, even though they were four miles away in the darkness: "That night, the boat was in the middle of the lake, and he was alone on land. He saw the disciples straining at the oars, because the wind was against them" (Mark 6:47–48 NIV). Closely related to this was Jesus' ability to see into the hearts of people some distance away (see John 1:47–48).

Charles Xavier frequently sent his own thoughts directly into another person's mind. This is also the chief way God speaks to His children. He rarely communicates in an audible voice, but rather speaks in a gentle, quiet voice, planting an impression in our minds that we should or should not do something. Sometimes He forms actual words in our consciousness. Many times, however, what we assume is God's voice is nothing more than our own thoughts (Jeremiah 23:21, 26), so we must be wary.

However, unlike Xavier, God doesn't completely take over people's mental faculties against their will, causing them to do or say something they normally wouldn't. When Magneto is about to kidnap Rogue in the movie *X-Men*, Xavier takes over one of Magneto's henchmen, using him like a puppet to try to force Magneto to stop. God, on the other hand, may come upon a person in great power, overwhelm his senses, and act through him, but *only* if he is already yielded to Him. We must grant Him permission.

Many people have the idea that since thoughts are barely detectable electrical impulses and minute synaptic sparks, that they're inconsequential nothings. They believe that if what they think doesn't actually hurt anyone, then it's their own private affair, and therefore nothing for God to be bothered about. But thoughts are real things. They aren't simply fleeting shadows of reality. They're the powerful generals that command your entire body.

God not only knows your thoughts, but He will one day judge you for whether you acted on your selfish impulses, or whether you failed to respond to noble, unselfish thoughts. A passing evil temptation won't ruin you as long as you resist it, just as a lustful thought won't corrupt you if you refuse to dwell on it and refrain from acting on it. So choose what you think about. As David prayed, "Let the words of my mouth, *and the meditation of my heart*, be acceptable in thy sight, O LORD, my strength, and my redeemer" (Psalm 19:14 KJV, emphasis added).

42. DEADLY THEOLOGY

In the first *X-Men* movie, Magneto arranges the kidnapping of his most outspoken adversary, Senator Robert Kelly. The Senator had constantly warned America about the danger of mutants, so, in a bizarre act of revenge, Magneto decides to transform *him* into a mutant. First, though, he asks, "Are you a God-fearing man, Senator? That is such a strange phrase. I've always thought of God as a teacher; a bringer of light, wisdom, and understanding."[119]

Like so many people, Magneto had come to the conclusion that fearing God was a negative concept, outdated and mistaken—that He was all light and acceptance and positive emotions. Yet despite his stated belief in such a God, Magneto was at that very moment involved in unimaginable evil.

As Magneto goes to turn on the mutation machine, the terrified Senator asks what he is about to do. Magneto replies, "Let's just say, God works too slow."[120] What he meant was that evolution—which he thought God had used to create mutants—had taken millions of years, but he was about to accelerate the process.

Magneto's reasoning sums up many people's philosophy. They believe that since "God is love" and "there is no fear in love" (1 John 4:8, 18 KJV), that He can't be associated with the "negative, judgmental deity" of the Old Testament, about whom it is written, "There is a God who judges the earth" (Psalm 58:11 NIV), and "God is greatly to be feared" (Psalm 89:7 KJV). And although Jesus is accepted as a great man whose teachings bring enlightenment, He had to have been mistaken when He said, "Be afraid of the One [God] who can destroy both soul and body in hell" (Matthew 10:28 NIV). According to this line of reasoning, an enlightened God would never judge and punish people in the afterlife.

Magneto came from a Jewish family whose parents were killed by the Nazis. Growing up in such a home, he would have been familiar with the Old Testament concept of a God of justice and judgment. Magneto probably didn't have a problem with God judging *his* enemies and bringing *him* justice when *he* had been wronged. But he'd come to the conclusion, likely because of the death of his parents, that "God works too slow."

In fact, Magneto probably would have agreed with the Jews in Zephaniah's day who said, "The LORD will not do good, neither will he do evil" (Zephaniah 1:12 KJV). Not only did God not act *immediately* when enemies needed to be judged, but many times He seemed not to act *at all*. A case in point: why didn't God stop Hitler and the Nazis from murdering millions of people? This question has deeply troubled many sincere believers from the 1930s till now.

The answer is that God *did* eventually stop the Nazis— and He used the Americans and their allies to accomplish this. God heard the desperate prayers of millions of suffering people and stirred up distant nations to fight for them— and to persevere in combat for years, at great personal cost—and eventually defeat this evil. Likewise, time and again in the Bible, when the Israelites faced oppression at the hands of their enemies, God inspired deliverers to rise up and also strengthened them in battle.

Seeing how God often uses *men* to bring about justice, many people mistakenly conclude that God isn't involved at all in helping them defeat evil, that many and desperate prayers have no impact on the situation. So they think they must take matters into their *own* hands if they want justice. Often God *does* call you to fight for what is right, but there are also times when you're powerless to deliver yourself from your own enemies. At times like these, God promises,

"It is mine to avenge; I will repay. In due time their foot will slip; their day of disaster is near" (Deuteronomy 32:35 NIV). It may take a while, but in time, *due time*, God will act.

The belief that God won't or can't do either good or evil motivates many people, just as Magneto's belief in a distant, barely involved deity drove him to a chilling attempt to commit global genocide. In *X-Men United*, he tries to use Charles Xavier and Cerebro to kill every human on Earth. Magneto attempted this precisely because he didn't fear God. Since he concluded that God wouldn't do a thing about his evil, in this life *or* in the next, he was sure that God wouldn't judge him.

How greatly he went astray! Although Magneto claimed to be guided by light and wisdom, it was his own twisted thirst for power and vengeance that drove him.

This is why it's wise to fear God. In fact, the Bible says, "The fear of the LORD is the beginning of wisdom" (Proverbs 9:10 KJV). Fearing God is not a negative thing. The Bible says, "The fear of the LORD is pure" (Psalm 19:9 NIV). Revering and fearing God motivates us to do good, knowing that "we will all stand before God's judgment seat" (Romans 14:10 NIV) to account for our deeds.

43. DISUNITY AND CIVIL WAR

In the 2012 movie *The Avengers*, Nick Fury explains the thinking behind the Avengers Initiative when he says, "The idea was to bring together a group of remarkable people to see if they could become something more. To see if they could work together. . .to fight the battles that we never could."[121] At first glance, it all sounds so easy: Because they were "remarkable people" and because they were the good guys, they'd naturally come together, each individual working selflessly for a common good, their powers melding seamlessly into one powerful force. Right?

In theory it sounds wonderful: a team of superheroes would be stronger and more effective than each of them working separately. The philosophy behind the Avengers' Initiative is in line with that of the Bible: "Two people are better off than one, for they can help each other succeed. If one person falls, the other can reach out and help. But someone who falls alone is in real trouble. . . . A person standing alone can be attacked and defeated, but two can stand back-to-back and conquer. Three are even better, for a triple-braided cord is not easily broken" (Ecclesiastes 4:9–10, 12 NLT).

However, Fury concedes that getting these superheroes to work together is a big "if." Bruce Banner (Hulk) doubts they can pull it off. Thinking about the raw power of each combatant, the large egos, the tendency to misunderstand, and short tempers, he doesn't have high hopes of them lasting long. He asks, "What are we, a team? No, no, no. We're a chemical mixture that makes chaos."[122] Elsewhere he describes the Avengers as a "freak show."[123] And yes, he *was* aware that as a rampaging green monster, he was the chief freak.

But there was hope. . .so long as they were willing to work together. As the group talks about stopping Ultron, Tony Stark asks how they could possibly accomplish it. Steve Rogers answered, "Together."[124]

Early on, some small cracks in their unity appear. Iron Man and Captain America criticize each other from the beginning—Iron Man constantly taking jabs at Cap's seemingly antiquated worldview and his efforts to police their foul language, and Cap constantly voicing his opinion about Iron Man's ego and overrated abilities. It comes as no surprise, therefore, that in the movie *Captain America: Civil War*, they lead pitched battles against each other, with Iron Man bluntly telling Cap, "Sometimes I want to punch you in your perfect teeth."[125]

Whenever you work with others in a team setting, there are benefits that make the sacrifices worthwhile, as well as built-in liabilities that can sink the whole ship. So you have to decide whether the benefits are worth it, whether you can put your pride aside to make the team work. You'll need to do that, because many people in the real world have large egos, short tempers, and a tendency to misunderstand.

And then there's the big question of who calls the shots. In the beginning, Iron Man has the good sense to step aside and recognize Captain America's leadership abilities. When Maria Hill refers to him as "boss," Iron Man points to Captain America and says, "Actually, *he's* the boss." But then he adds, "I just pay for everything, and design everything, make everyone look cooler."[126] He just can't resist stating that he deserves the credit for keeping the whole show on the road.

Major confrontations can often erupt over very small incidents, but often there are larger issues simmering beneath the surface, and a small incident is simply the spark that causes it all to explode. This was the case in ancient Israel: David's son Absalom had risen against him but was defeated in war. With Absalom dead, the northern tribes of Israel began speaking of bringing the king back to Jerusalem.

But the men of Judah beat them to it. Shortly after they had ferried King David across the Jordan River, the Israelites showed up, wanting to know why Judah hadn't allowed them to help. They said, "We have ten shares in the king; therefore we also have more right to David than you. Why then do you despise us—were we not the first to advise bringing back our king?" But then the Bible gives these telling words: "Yet the words of the men of Judah were fiercer than the words of the men of Israel" (2 Samuel 19:43 NKJV).

The men of Judah won the argument that day by arguing more angrily and fiercely than the Israelites, but their "victory" came with a huge price tag. It so happened that a man named Sheba was there. He blew a trumpet and said, "We have *no* share in David. . .every man to his tents, O Israel!" (2 Samuel 20:1 NKJV, emphasis added). All the Israelites deserted David—and the civil war was on. . .*again*.

Beware of "small issues" of pride and rivalry. They may seem insignificant at first, but they can become major issues during times of great strain and testing—such as the Avengers faced in the *Civil War* film. These issues can grow until they destroy unity and undermine the good a team could otherwise accomplish.

44. IMMORTAL WARRIORS

Several superheroes have been around so long that fans question why they never age. Wolverine was born in the 1880s—in the 1830s according to the opening scene of *X-Men Origins: Wolverine*—but he's still going strong. Nick Fury was born in the early 1920s, was the leader of a commando team in World War II, but is still kicking. Black Widow (Natasha) was born during the late 1930s, yet still has the beauty and vitality of a woman in her twenties. How does Marvel explain such anomalies?

They actually have explanations. According to the comicbooks, Nick Fury was badly injured by a land mine near the end of WWII. While caring for Fury, a French scientist used him as a test subject for his Infinity Formula.

The formula healed him, granting Fury greatly extended health and energy. Plus it halted his aging.

As for Natasha, while she was training in the Soviet "Red Room Academy," she was biotechnologically enhanced—exactly how, we aren't told—giving her exceptionally long life and youthful appearance.

When it comes to Wolverine, need you ask? His most outstanding mutant power is a tremendously accelerated healing process that regenerates damaged or destroyed body tissues. Not surprisingly, this healing ability also inhibits aging, enabling him to live far longer than most men. Although he's about 180 years old, Wolverine has the appearance and vitality of a man in his prime. In the 2009 movie *X-Men: Origins*, William Stryker asks him, "After defending this country for 150 years. . .how would you like to *really* serve your country?"[127]

But about here we should ask the question, "Is such longevity, together with undiminished health, feasible, or is it just the stuff of comicbooks?" The answer to this is found in another question: "Did biblical patriarchs actually live hundreds of years?" Until just a few years ago, many people responded with incredulity when they read of the ancient patriarchs living for centuries. (Some still do!) After all, according to the Bible, Methuselah died when he was 969 years old (see Genesis 5:27).

In recent years, however, microbiologists and molecular

geneticists have learned that aging is largely caused by accumulative damage to our DNA and are exploring molecular repair and rejuvenation of deteriorated cells and tissues in an effort to extend the human lifespan. Also, as reported in the January, 2009 issue of *National Geographic*, when *Turritopsis dohrnii*, the "immortal jellyfish," is wounded, sick, or old, it can revert to an immature polyp by changing all its cells into a younger state. Theoretically, it could continue doing this indefinitely—achieving near immortality.

But for the moment, let's consider just rejuvenating cells—making every old, diseased, and damaged cell in your body young and healthy again. It may be possible. Researchers are confident that they'll eventually be able to stop the aging process so that humans can live hundreds or—according to some optimists—even thousands of years. Suddenly the idea of patriarchs living for centuries doesn't seem so incredible.

Many Christians believe that thousands of years ago, mankind's DNA was much stronger and wasn't as easily damaged or susceptible to aging. They believe that, among other things, the Earth's magnetic field was stronger and shielded it from most ultraviolet radiation. But after the Flood, the shielding was greatly diminished, damage to the DNA began to accumulate, and lifespans began to shorten. According to the Bible, Shem lived

600 years; Arphaxad 438 years; Peleg 239 years; Terah 205 years; Abraham 175 years, Jacob 147 years; Joseph 110 years, and so on (see Genesis 11:10–26, 32; 25:7; 47:28; 50:26).

But if scientists could find the "switch" in human DNA, they could, theoretically, slow down or even reverse this process. This is similar to what Wolverine does every time his body rapidly heals. This also helps us grasp what Jesus accomplished when He instantly healed tens of thousands of people. Since Jesus used the power of the Spirit of God, we can't fully understand how He did these things, but at least we know that an explanation exists—even if it's still beyond us.

For centuries, people have sought eternal youth by natural means. In the sixteenth century, Spanish explorer Ponce de León searched for the mythical Fountain of Youth in Florida. While his efforts may seem naive to us today, God is the One who put this desire for eternal life in the heart of man: "He has also set eternity in the human heart" (Ecclesiastes 3:11 NIV).

And the good news is this: God is more than happy to give you eternal life! David prayed, "You will prolong the king's life, his years as many generations. He shall abide before God forever" (Psalm 61:6–7 NKJV). And how do you get it? By receiving Jesus Christ as your Savior. Jesus Himself said, "Whoever believes in the Son has eternal life, but whoever rejects the Son will not see life" (John 3:36 NIV). And the apostle John promised, "The world and its desires pass away, but whoever does the will of God lives forever" (1 John 2:17 NIV).

T HOR

45. ABOVE THIS DARK WORLD

In the movie, *Thor: The Dark World*, ages ago, Bor, Thor's grandfather, fought the armies of Malekith the Dark Elf on Svartalfheim, the Dark World. Malekith had sought to use the Aether, an ancient force capable of immeasurable destruction, to transform the entire universe into unending night. But Bor defeated the Dark Elves, and thinking them all dead, he hid the Aether on Svartalfheim. Unknown to him, however, Malekith and part of his army had escaped.

In the present time, the Convergence, a rare alignment of the Nine Realms, is about to happen, and as it approaches, portals linking the worlds begin to appear. In London, astrophysicist Jane Foster comes across one such portal in an abandoned factory. She is swept through the gateway into the dark world, where the Aether, seeking a host, enters her. (The Aether was one of six Infinity Stones, but, unlike the other gems, it wasn't always in solid form.) Jane wakes up back on Earth several hours later. When Thor finds her and realizes she isn't well, he carries her away to Asgard to be healed.

Malekith, sensing that the Aether had stirred again and is in Asgard, sends his harrows (starships) there. Similar to the Star Wars movies, *Thor: The Dark World* portrays pitched battles utilizing a mixture of laser cannons and arms blazing searing pulses of light, along with swords and other seemingly primitive weapons. For personal combat, the Asgardian warriors definitely favor ancient weapons over phasers. Malekith's attack wreaks havoc in Valhalla before he is finally forced to withdraw.

Then Thor, Loki, and Jane, determined to lead Malekith away from Asgard before he attacks again, flee to the dark world. Malekith follows them there and, after capturing Jane, draws the Aether out of her and into himself, then leaves for Earth, intent on plunging the universe into darkness during the Convergence. But Thor and Jane discover a portal back to Earth and pursue him. Thor and Malekith then battle, appearing and disappearing between several worlds. Finally, Thor sends Malekith to the dark world, where he is crushed by his own ship.

The difference between Asgard and Svartalfheim could hardly be more striking. When Thor took Jane up to his father's realm, she was in awe of the surpassing beauty of Valhalla, capitol of this heavenly world. It was filled with life and light and splendor. Standing on a high balcony, surrounded by blossom-festooned branches and gazing out over the city, all Jane can do is whisper, "Wow!"[128]

Asgard was the Viking equivalent of the Christian heaven, but a pale shadow of the biblical reality. But the breathtaking scenes in the movie are how many Christians envision "the city of the living God, the heavenly Jerusalem" (Hebrews 12:22 NKJV). The apostle John describes it like this: "The Holy City, Jerusalem. . . shone with the glory of God, and its brilliance was like that of a very precious jewel, like a jasper, clear as crystal. . . . The wall was made of jasper, and the city of pure gold, as pure as glass. The foundations of the city walls were decorated with every kind of precious stone" (Revelation 21:10–11, 18–19 NIV).

By contrast, Svartalfheim was a gloomy, arid, desolate realm, filled with the wreckage of battle and the ghosts of long-dead Dark Elves. A star that resembled a black hole scowled in the sullen sky above, shedding only dim light on the forsaken world below. The Bible describes hell in different ways, but three times Jesus described it as "outer darkness" (Matthew 22:13 NKJV) and Jude wrote that the wicked were "wandering stars for whom is reserved the blackness of darkness forever" (Jude 1:13 NKJV). Jesus also described an "unclean spirit" who "goes through dry places, seeking rest, and finds none" (Matthew 12:43 NKJV).

And yes, the Bible also describes Satan making an attack on heaven, similar to that of Malekith and his forces on Valhalla: "Then war broke out in heaven. Michael and his angels fought against the dragon, and the dragon and his angels fought back. But he was not strong enough, and they lost their place in heaven. The great dragon was hurled down—that ancient serpent called the devil, or Satan, who leads the whole world astray. He was hurled to the earth, and his angels with him" (Revelation 12:7–9 NIV).

In the past, several Dark Elves had allowed Cursed Stones to be implanted within their bodies, transforming them into super warriors. At terrible personal cost, these stones morphed them into the Kursed, twisted demonic beings—taller, larger, more powerful, and more grotesque. In the movie, Algrim, Malekith's lieutenant, agrees to accept the final Stone and become the last Kursed. As he inserts the stone, Malekith tells him, "You will become darkness, cursed to this existence until it consumes you."[129]

How much better to be to filled with God's light,

empowered by His Holy Spirit, and destined to eternal life in His glorious heavenly city above: "For you were once darkness, but now you are light in the Lord. Walk as children of light" (Ephesians 5:8 NKJV). It should fill you with great peace to know that God has destined you for paradise forever.

46. DEFYING THE DEVIL

One comicbook in particular preached the Gospel to me during my youth. I was fifteen when *Silver Surfer* issue 3, titled *The Power and the Prize*, came out in December, 1968. In this story, a powerful, diabolical being named Mephisto, lord of the lower depths, gloated over how he had so corrupted mankind that their lost souls were being swept by the millions into his kingdom. (Mephisto is one of the chief demons of German literature, and Marvel artist John Buscema illustrated him like a dark Faustian devil.)

But there was a threat. Seldom in the history of the world had Mephisto sensed such goodness of soul, such purity of spirit as he now sensed within the Silver Surfer, and he realized that as long as the Silver Surfer existed, his plans for the damnation of mankind would be in jeopardy. So the cunning demon became determined to corrupt him.

Mephisto knew that Silver Surfer was originally a mortal from the distant planet of Zenn-La named Norrin Radd, and that he had been forced to leave behind his true love, the beautiful Shalla-bal. Knowing that Silver Surfer still yearned for her, Mephisto lured her to Earth in a spacecraft. Then he confronted Silver Surfer, offering him the desire of his heart in exchange for his allegiance. Mephisto insisted, "Your soul must be mine." He wanted him in his domain, saying, "There shall I bend you to my Satanic will."[130]

Silver Surfer refused, so Mephisto swept Shalla-bal away to the stygian underworld. When Silver Surfer followed them, Mephisto began his temptations. First he offered Silver Surfer a vast hoard of jewels and gold if he would serve him, telling him that wealth such as no living mortal had ever possessed would be his. But Silver Surfer scorned his treasure and let him know he wasn't tempted.

Then Mephisto, guessing that Silver Surfer was attracted to Shalla-bal's exquisite beauty, offered him not one, but three breathtakingly gorgeous, desirable women. But again he refused. Finally, Mephisto showed him a vision of a mighty civilization spanning countless star systems, and promised the Surfer that if he would but say the word, a galactic empire would call him king for all ages. But again Silver Surfer resisted.

Then Mephisto played his final card. He threatened to send Shalla-bal back to distant Zenn-La, knowing that Silver Surfer, who was confined to Earth, would never see her again. If he wanted to be united with his true love, he had to kneel before Mephisto. Otherwise he would lose Shalla-bal forever.

In an incredibly touching scene, while the man she loved hesitated, Shalla-bal cried out for him not to give in. She posed a haunting question: "How can love have meaning— if it costs your very soul?"[131] In so saying, she was all but quoting the words of Jesus, who asked, "For what profit is it to a man if he gains the whole world, and loses his own soul?" (Matthew 16:26 NKJV).

It's obvious that the writer was attempting to smuggle the Gospel into this story, and that he was making little effort to hide it, for Mephisto's temptations of Silver Surfer closely mirror Satan's temptations of Christ (Matthew 4:1–11): "Then Jesus was led up by the Spirit into the wilderness to be tempted by the devil. . . . Now when the tempter came to Him, he said, 'If You are the Son of God, command that these stones become bread" (vss. 1–3). Jesus refused to yield to this temptation, but then, "the devil took Him up into the holy city, set Him on the pinnacle of the temple, and said to Him, "If You are the Son of God, throw Yourself down" (vs. 7). Once again, Jesus resisted.

Finally, "the devil took Him up on an exceedingly high mountain, and showed Him all the kingdoms of the world and their glory. And he said to Him, 'All these things I will give You if You will fall down and worship me.' Then Jesus said to him, 'Away with you, Satan! For it is written, "You shall worship the Lord your God, and Him only you shall serve."' Then the devil left Him" (vss. 8–11).

Hebrews tells us, "We do not have a High Priest who cannot sympathize with our weaknesses, but was in all points tempted as we are, yet without sin" (Hebrews 4:15 NKJV). Jesus proved that it *is* possible to resist Satan's temptations, no matter how alluring they may be. Paul tells us, "No temptation has overtaken you except what is common to mankind. And God is faithful; he will not let you be tempted beyond what you can bear" (1 Corinthians 10:13 NIV). Whether you're being tempted by riches, illicit sex, power, or anything else, God can help you stand strong.

Jesus commanded, "Away with you, Satan!" and Silver Surfer cried out, "I defy you, Mephisto! Darkness must ever retreat before the light!"[132] This is true, and you, too, can defy the evil one and stand strong in Christ. The Bible says, "Resist the devil, and he *will* flee from you" (James 4:7 NIV, emphasis added).

47. FALSE GODS AND CHRISTS

In popular usage, the word *apocalypse* means the ultimate, utter destruction of the world. But originally it meant "an uncovering of something hidden; a lifting of the veil." In the 2016 movie *X-Men: Apocalypse*, the revelation is that the supervillain Apocalypse was the ultimate answer to a question most people hadn't even thought to ask: where did all of Earth's gods originate? According to Marvel, since the birth of human civilization, the super-mutant Apocalypse was worshiped as a god, and in the movie he claims, "I've been called many things over many lifetimes—Ra, Krishna, Yahweh. I was there to spark and fan the flame of man's awakening. . ."[133]

This is pure fiction, of course. As you may know, Yahweh

is the personal name of the Hebrew God, usually replaced by the word LORD (in small caps) in most Bible translations. The Holman Christian Standard Bible is one of few translations that spells out the divine name. Unbelieving scholars have long insisted that Yahweh was originally a minor deity, worshiped by desert tribes known as the Shashu (Midianites/Edomites), and only later incorporated into the Hebrew religion. But this isn't true. The Midianites and Edomites were descended from the Hebrews and learned of Yahweh from them.

Saying that Yahweh began as a powerful mutant is simply giving a new twist to an old idea. It's more in line with modern theories, however. Some people believe that early man mistakenly worshiped extraterrestrials as deities. This is what Erich von Däniken postulated in his 1968 book *Chariots of the Gods*. Appearances of the Egyptian god Ra, the Hindu god Krishna, as well as the Hebrew God Yahweh, are all explained as encounters with superior beings—or, in *X-Men: Apocalypse*, as the supreme mutant, Apocalypse.

According to Marvel comic lore, Apocalypse was the Earth's earliest and most powerful mutant, a former mortal who absorbed the powers of many other mutants and became invincible and immortal. Upon awakening after thousands of years, Apocalypse gathered a team of potent mutants to purify mankind and create a new world order, with him as its guiding light. It was then up to Professor X and Raven to lead the X-Men and save mankind.

In the movie, Moira tells Alex Summers that, down through history, Apocalypse always had four followers to whom he gave great power. This time they are Psylocke, Archangel, Storm, and Magneto. Alex notes, "Like the Four Horsemen of the Apocalypse. He got that one from the Bible." Moira counters, "Or the Bible got it from him."[134] This is what many people believe: that the Bible borrowed all of its ideas—including the concept of God Himself—from pagan sources.

In other Marvel comics, a mighty feminine power arose who called herself "Goddess." Many superheroes readily accepted her as a manifestation of the Supreme Being. Goddess stated, "I will contact and awaken the Holy Spirit in every enlightened being in the heavens. I shall guide this collected consciousness to true bliss and holy salvation."[135] She spoke of "spreading this Gospel"[136] and declared, "I am the Way,"[137] just as Jesus said in John 14:6. She claimed, "Only I. . .can rescue humanity and mutantkind from eternal Hell's fire."[138]

You may be surprised that a so-called deity or false prophet would boldly repeat biblical truths and expressions and claim that he or she is fulfilling them, but it's more prevalent than you might imagine. Today, a number of formerly mainline churches practice Gaia-worship and have opened themselves to belief in a great feminine goddess, all the while cloaking such heresies in the language of the Bible. Many people are susceptible to such beliefs. This is why Paul admonished the first Christians, "If he who comes preaches another Jesus whom we have not preached, or if you receive a different spirit which you have not received, or a different gospel which you have not accepted—you may well put up with it!" (2 Corinthians 11:4 NKJV).

How can you avoid "putting up with it?" How can you keep from being deceived by such false teachings? The key is to know your Bible well. Be aware of the Bible prophesies that these things will happen in the last days so you can avoid being taken in. Jesus warned, "Many will come in My name, saying, 'I am the Christ,' and will deceive many" (Matthew 24:5 NKJV). False teachers may come teaching secret knowledge, "Satan's so-called deep secrets" (Revelation 2:24 NIV), usually just to try to convince you that someone other than Yahweh is God.

The following verses reveal the power and greatness of the one true God: "Who is God besides Yahweh? And who is a rock? Only our God" (Psalm 18:31 HCSB). "Ascribe to Yahweh the glory due His name; worship Yahweh in the splendor of His holiness" (Psalm 29:2 HCSB). "For Yahweh, the Most High, is awe-inspiring, a great King over all the earth" (Psalm 47:2 HCSB). "My soul, praise Yahweh! LORD my God, You are very great; You are clothed with majesty and splendor" (Psalm 104:1 HCSB). "I know that Yahweh is great; our Lord is greater than all gods" (Psalm 135:5 HCSB).

GHOST RIDER

48. OVERCOMING DEMONS

Would it surprise you to learn that demons such as Satan, Lucifer, Beelzeboul (Beelzebub), Mephisto, and Ba'al appear in Marvel Comics as supervillains? Well, they and other fallen evil spirits have appeared frequently fighting superheroes. . .and each other. The demon Mephisto (aka Roarke) was featured prominently in the movie *Ghost Rider* (2007).

Most critics gave the film negative reviews, but that didn't stop the producers from making a sequel, *Ghost Rider: Spirit of Vengeance* (2011), which received even worse marks. Like *Spawn* (1997) before them, the movies didn't do a good job presenting how to deal with evil spirits.

In the first film, Mephisto makes an offer to teen motorcycle stunt rider Johnny Blaze: he'd cure his father of cancer if Blaze would sell him his soul. The youth agrees, and the next day, his dad's cancer is gone—but he dies a few hours later in a fiery motorcycle accident. Blaze accuses Mephisto of tricking him, but the demon insists that he'd fulfilled his part of the contract. But an old man named the Caretaker tells Blaze, "Any man that's got the guts to sell his soul for love. . .did it for the right reason. Maybe that puts God on your side."[139] This is a dangerous deception.

Years later, Mephisto's renegade son Blackheart comes to Earth to retrieve the contract of San Venganza, hidden by a cowboy who'd been known as the Ghost Rider. Mephisto offers Blaze his soul back if he'll stop Blackheart and bring *him* the contract. He then empowers Blaze with the evil spirit, Zarathos, making him the new Ghost Rider and causing his motorcycle and body to burn with yellow flames. Blaze defeats Blackheart, but when Mephisto wants to return Blaze's soul to him, Blaze foolishly refuses, saying that he'd use his new powers to fight Mephisto and avenge all evil.

By the second movie, Johnny Blaze has become a reckless dispenser of justice, punishing both great crimes and small mistakes equally. Then a French priest, Moreau, promises Blaze that if he'll protect a young boy from Mephisto, Moreau would exorcize the evil spirit possessing Blaze and get rid of his contract. Blaze protects the boy and Moreau keeps his bargain and drives the demon from him.

But when Mephisto attacks him, Blaze allows Zarathos to empower him again, and then defeats Mephisto. Then Zarathos changes. He'd originally been an angel, the Spirit of Justice, but he had been tricked into entering Hell, where he'd gone insane and been turned into the Spirit of Vengeance. He now reverts to being an angel. Glowing with pure blue flame, Johnnie Blaze rides off, a righteous Ghost Rider.

Not likely. Demons don't change into angels. They may pretend to be an "angel of light" (2 Corinthians 11:14 KJV), but it's only a deception. The devil is "a liar, and the father of it" (John 8:44 KJV). Even in Marvel comic lore, Lucifer is called "The Prince of Lies."

It's fallacious to believe that people can outwit the devil and use his own power to fight him—fighting fire with fire—or to believe that as long as you have good motives, you'll be okay. That isn't so. Paul wrote, "Do not give the devil a foothold" (Ephesians 4:27 NIV). God is the only One who can give you power over evil. Jesus "called His twelve disciples together and gave them power and authority over all demons" (Luke 9:1 NKJV).

But the movie-makers did get some things right:

according to comic lore, demons are bound by very specific rules. For example, they can't force people to yield to them; they only gain power when men willingly surrender to them, and they're masters at using lies and deceit to trick people into doing this.

In the comicbooks, people make deals with the devil to gain selfish benefits, signing a contract to sell their souls. But people don't need to sign a literal contract to lose their soul to him. They must simply choose to do evil day after day, until they become fully entrenched in it, or they can dabble in what they think are "small" sins until the habit grows out of control. The apostle Paul wrote, "You cannot drink from the cup of the Lord and from the cup of demons, too. You cannot eat at the Lord's Table and at the table of demons, too" (1 Corinthians 10:21 NLT). If you try to, evil will overthrow you.

But the good news is, God can deliver even the most hopeless sinner and set him or her free from evil. Mary Magdalene was possessed by seven devils, but Jesus cast them out and totally restored her life. She then drew so close to Jesus that she was the first person to see Him after His resurrection from the dead (see Mark 16:9; John 20:10–18). God has saved countless souls from darkness since that day: "He has rescued us from the dominion of darkness and brought us into the kingdom of the Son he loves" (Colossians 1:13 NIV).

The devil will still try to tempt and deceive you, but the Bible says, "Put on the full armor of God, so that you can take your stand against the devil's schemes" (Ephesians 6:11 NIV).

49. PROGRAMMING AND COMPASSION

Almost invariably, superheroes appear first in comicbooks, and if they prove to be popular, they move on to the big screen. However, the movie *RoboCop*, which came out in 1987, inspired comicbook spinoffs—first a one-shot Marvel Comics adaptation of the film that year, followed by a 23-issue series (1990–1992).

In 2014, director José Padilha did a powerful remake of *RoboCop*. His movie is set in Chicago in 2028, when technology had allowed cybernetics to interface almost seamlessly with humans. Robots are keeping the peace in most of the world, but the Dreyfuss Act prohibits cybernetic policing in America. As Senator Dreyfuss argues, "A machine...can't understand the value of human life. Why should it be allowed to take one? To legislate over life and death, we need people who understand right from wrong."[140]

The multinational company OmniCorp circumvents this legal obstacle by putting a man inside a robot. OmniCorp chose police detective Alex Murphy, who had been killed by a car bomb. Most of Alex's body was badly burned and all his internal organs, except for his lungs, were irreparably damaged. Even parts of his brain were destroyed. Dr. Dennett Norton revives Alex and puts his head inside a machine. Then Dr. Norton tells Alex, "We had to repair the damaged areas, but we didn't interfere with your emotion or your intellect. . . . You're in control."[141]

That's what he told *Alex*. But he tells OmniCorp executives, "The human element will always be present. Fear, instinct, bias, compassion—they will always interfere with the system."[142] To prevent the "human element" from "interfering," he drastically reduces the levels of dopamine in Alex's brain, which allows the software to take over and make decisions, thus transforming him into a lethal fighting machine with super-quick reflexes. Alex's human side is basically just along for the ride.

However, when Alex's wife tells him about the trauma their son had been suffering (the boy had witnessed the explosion that killed his father), Alex manages to override his programming and drive to his house, where he taps into the close-circuit cameras and witnesses his own fiery death. In the end, Alex solves his own murder and exposes corruption inside the Chicago Police Department.

There's an important lesson here for believers: it's good to have doctrine, and the apostles spent quite a bit of time in the New Testament informing us about the difference between true and false teachings, but like OmniCorp, religious people are sometimes guilty of manufacturing their own doctrines—their own programming—that override the clear commands of God and the voice of His Spirit.

Dr. Norton points out that "compassion. . .will always interfere with the system," and OmniCorp sees this as a problem. So did the Pharisees in Jesus' day. They were constantly creating doctrines that shut down love and compassion. Jesus told them, "You have a fine way of setting aside the commands of God in order to observe your own traditions! For Moses said, 'Honor your father and mother'. . . . But you say that if anyone declares that what might have been used to help their father or mother is Corban (that is, devoted to God)—then you no longer let them do anything for their father or mother. Thus you nullify the word of God by your tradition" (Mark 7:9–13 NIV).

Jesus stated that the greatest commandments are to love God with all your heart and to love others. John stated that whoever sees a fellow believer in need but turns away and shows no compassion clearly lacks love (1 John 3:17). The Pharisees obviously had low dopamine levels. They went through the motions of being meticulously righteous and obedient to God, but they lacked compassion and mercy.

Do you ever allow the mental programming of doctrine to shut down your compassion? If you're asked to help impoverished children in war-ravaged or drought-stricken countries, do you automatically assure yourself that you don't need to give because "God is judging that nation for their sins, so let them stew in their own juice"? Or if someone asks you to help them with a project, is your reaction, "Everyone is responsible to make their *own* way in life"? Or when you're asked to forgive someone, do you tell yourself, "I will if they're *truly* sorry"—and then never accept their contrition as genuine?

Of course, you can't give to *every* need and you can't help *everyone* who asks you to lend a hand, but if you *can* help, you should seriously consider doing so: "Do not withhold good from those to whom it is due, when it is in the power of your hand to do so" (Proverbs 3:27 NKJV). Override any self-centered programming today and allow God's love and compassion to motivate you.

50. ON EARTH FOR A REASON

The four *Superman* movies starring Christopher Reeve (1978–87) are established classics and, in the essentials, stay true to the well-known story of the man from Krypton. But the 2013 movie *Man of Steel* (2013), with Henry Cavill as Superman, is a powerful remake, even though it deviates from the traditional script—or perhaps I should say, *because* it deviates. After all, Superman is such a well-known story that, told straight up, it can be boring.

Here are the basics: Superman's home planet, Krypton, is about to explode, its core weakened and unstable, so his father Jor-El seeks to save his son's life by sending him away from the doomed planet. The interstellar capsule arrives on Earth and lands in a field in Kansas. Jonathan and Martha Kent find the capsule and raise the boy as their own son, Clark Kent.

Earth's weaker gravity, richer atmosphere, and yellow sun, give Clark extraordinary powers. As he grows to manhood, he begins manifesting superhuman strength. In fact, he eventually has such *great* powers, and so *many* different ones, that he is utterly invincible. His father Jor-El had predicted, "He'll be a god to them."[143] Sure enough, in the comics, no one on Earth stood a chance against him. This necessitated arming nearly every villain with Kryptonite (which comes from radioactive meteorites from Krypton) to strip Superman of his powers. Plus, it seemed that the major subplot in every movie is Lois Lane trying to find out his secret identity.

Director Zack Snyder's *Man of Steel* had the second subplot, but the genius of his film was adding deep layers of troubling emotions and a sense of isolation to the familiar story. *Man of Steel* highlights Clark's sense of being different from other kids as well as his fear and confusion over his developing powers.

Plus, his adoptive father, Jonathan Kent, had advised him not to reveal his powers, even to save life or to defend himself. Although this seems excessive, doing good anonymously turned out to have been a wise path that allowed Superman to mature in his powers before being put to the test. As Clark later says, "My father believed that if the world found out who I really was, they'd reject me. . .out of fear."[144] So for a long time, Clark travels around the country under assumed names, quietly doing good and saving lives.

This film also emphasizes a deep sense of destiny. Just before sending his infant son to Earth, Jor-El had embedded the complete genetic codex of the people of Krypton into his cells. The entire future and hope of Krypton rests on Clark's shoulders. In addition, he is destined to be a shining light to mankind. As Jor-El's holographic persona tells his now-grown son, he would give the people of Earth an ideal to strive toward, and he would help them accomplish amazing things.[145]

The parallel between Superman's father sending his son to Earth and God the Father sending His Son Jesus to Earth is clear. Jesus repeatedly said, "the Father has sent Me" (John 5:36 NKJV), and John records Him telling Nicodemus, "God did not send His Son into the world to condemn the world, but that the world through Him might be saved" (John 3:17 NKJV).

In *Man of Steel*, Superman's mother, Lara Lor-Van, could have been describing Jesus' destiny when she predicts her own son's future, saying, "He will be an outcast. They'll kill him."[146] The Bible tells us about Jesus: "He was in the world. . .and the world did not know Him. He came to His own, and His own did not receive Him" (John 1:10–11 NKJV). Also, Peter told the people of Jerusalem, "You nailed him to a cross and killed him." But the good news is, "God. . .raised him back to life, for death could not keep him in its grip" (Acts 2:24 NLT).

Jesus said, "I am the light of the world" (John 8:12 NLT), and if His Spirit dwells in your heart, then you too have God's light, despite how weak and unworthy you may feel at times. The more you seek to follow Jesus and put His teachings into practice in your daily life, doing good and helping others whenever you can, the more you become a shining light showing others the way. This is why Jesus could say, "You are the light of the world. . . . let your good deeds shine out for all to see, so that everyone will praise your heavenly Father" (Matthew 5:14, 16 NLT). At the same time, however, you can also expect to be misunderstood and rejected at times—just as Jesus was.

Like Clark Kent, you might be living in obscurity, your good deeds largely unseen. But don't be discouraged: if you have faith in Jesus, you have a great destiny. You too were sent here for a reason. Sooner or later, you'll have your day in the sun, that day when all the good you've done will be recognized. Until that day, be faithful to the truth.

51. OVERCOMING FEAR

Batman Begins (2005) was the first movie in The Dark Knight Trilogy and was acclaimed by *Forbes*, *Rolling Stone*, and *Newsarama* as the top superhero movie of all time. Fear is a common theme throughout, and it begins with Bruce Wayne as a child falling into a dry well where bats swarmed him, terrifying him. Not long after, a mugger kills his parents. Fourteen years later, the killer is released from prison for agreeing to testify against Carmine Falcone, Gotham City's top crime boss.

Now a young adult, Bruce seeks revenge, but before he can act, Falcone has the mugger killed. When Bruce confronts Falcone, the mob boss boasts that his *real* power comes from being feared. Falcone informs him, "This is a world you'll never understand. And you always fear what you don't understand."[147]

Bruce then sets out on a long quest, traveling the world, to understand the criminal mind and to conquer his fears, and he ends up in Bhutan, where the villain Ra's al Ghul trains him as a member of the League of Shadows. Bruce *did* master his fears and learn fighting skills, but when he discovers that the League plans to destroy Gotham, believing it to be hopelessly corrupt, he returns to America to save the city.

Once back in the US, Bruce takes over his father's business, Wayne Enterprises, and the company's leading scientist, Lucius Fox, supplies him with impressive technology—a heavily armored car and a bulletproof body suit. Bruce then creates the persona of Batman to strike fear into the hearts of criminals, stating, "Bats frighten me. It's time my enemies shared my dread."[148]

Then Wayne discovers that a corrupt psychopharmacologist, Dr. Jonathan Crane (aka the Scarecrow), is working for Ra's al Ghul and has spiked Gotham's water supply with a fear-inducing hallucinogenic drug. Once it is airborne and inhaled, the drug will cause mass hysteria and drive people to violence, destroying the city. Batman thwarts the League's plans, however, and Gotham is spared.

One reason this movie resonates so deeply with

viewers is that the plot, at its heart, is similar to actual terror plots in the world today: a small group of extremists form a conspiracy to bomb a public place or attack crowded venues with automatic weapons. On September 11, 2001, terrorists attacked New York with passenger jets, bringing down the Twin Towers and causing great loss of life. Death and destruction is often only the terrorists' secondary goal; the *primary* goal is to cause psychological trauma, to weaken a nation's resolve and to cause people to give up in fear.

You probably haven't suffered directly from the effects of a terrorist attack, but you may have experienced the disabling effects of fear the constant attacks in this nation and around the world has caused so many others—or you may feel fear over events in your own life. Like Bruce Wayne, you may suffer from a phobia. Or you might suffer from the most primal fear of all—the fear of death, and the uncertainty of what will happen to your soul after you die.

Defeating such fear is one of the reasons Jesus died on the Cross. He died to save you from your sins, but He also died "that through death He might destroy him who had the power of death, that is, the devil, and release those who through fear of death were all their lifetime subject to bondage" (Hebrews 2:14–15 NKJV).

In *Batman Begins*, Dr. Crane uses a scarecrow mask

to frighten people. In reality, a scarecrow is lifeless and can't do anything to anybody. The most it can accomplish is to *appear* to be alive and scare crows away from a cornfield. By contrast, the threat Ra's al Ghul poses in the movie, and the threats real-life terrorists pose, are very real and very serious. There are many scarecrows in the world today, so it pays to differentiate between real threats and imaginary ones—and to face them both with courage and faith in God.

All "fear involves torment," but don't forget, "There is no fear in love; but perfect love casts out fear" (1 John 4:18 NKJV). If you feel fear, you can know for certain that it's not of God, "For God has not given us a spirit of fear, but of power and of love and of a sound mind" (2 Timothy 1:7 NKJV). So how can you have a sound mind, free from phobias, anxieties, and paranoia? How can anyone experience power in the face of threats and danger? By loving God and trusting in Him.

Everyone experiences fear from time to time, even believers. The question is: how do you respond? When the Philistines seized David and he thought he was about to be killed, he felt fear. But he made a choice to trust God to protect him, and said, "When I am afraid, I will put my trust in You" (Psalm 56:3 NASB). If you've already put your trust in God, continue to trust Him steadfastly, without wavering.

WONDER WOMAN

52. AMAZONS OF GOD

Wonder Woman is a princess of the Amazons—female warriors of Greek mythology—and in her homeland she bears the title Princess Diana of Themyscira. Since the 1980s, Diana has been known as the daughter of Zeus, king of the Greek gods, so it's likely that most of her amazing powers stem directly from this heritage.

Since her creation in 1941, Wonder Woman has been depicted as being as strong as Superman—so strong, in fact, that she once lifted a 50,000-pound rock above her head. She has an incredible range of combat skills and powers: she's bulletproof and has super wisdom, telescopic vision, and super hearing. During the 1960s, she gained even *more* powers, such as super breath and telepathy. She can also fly at half the speed of light.

With her many, many superpowers, Wonder Woman is considerably more powerful than ordinary mortals. Yet in the 1970s TV series starring Lynda Carter, she had few powers. It was refreshing to see her returned to her full glory and power on the big screen in the 2016 movie *Batman vs. Superman*. In it, Bruce Wayne tells Diana, "I've known a few women like you," and she tartly replies, "Oh, I don't think you've ever known a woman like me."[149] Little did Bruce know how true her words were.

In addition to her powers, Wonder Woman has three main weapons. Anyone she ropes with her Lasso of Truth (the Lariat of Hestia) is compelled to tell the truth. She also has a pair of indestructible bracelets, which she often uses to deflect bullets. Finally, she has a tiara she can hurl like a boomerang. With her great might and wisdom, Wonder Woman has long been the most outstanding comicbook heroine and a champion of gender equality.

The Bible boasts powerful women as well. Deborah was the judge of Israel in a patriarchal society in which women normally had no say in governing. But people throughout the land recognized Deborah's wisdom, and because the Spirit of God was upon her, men came from far and wide to seek her counsel. She was a prophetess;

God gave her divine wisdom to judge difficult cases and revealed the future to her (Judges 4:4–5).

At that time, the armies of Jabin, a powerful Canaanite king, were oppressing the northern tribes of Israel. So one day Deborah sent for Barak, a renowned warrior, and when he appeared before her, she said, "This is what the LORD, the God of Israel, commands you: Call out 10,000 warriors from the tribes of Naphtali and Zebulun at Mount Tabor. And I will call out Sisera, commander of Jabin's army, along with his chariots and warriors, to the Kishon River. There I will give you victory over him" (Judges 4:6–7 NLT).

Barak replied, "I will go, but only if you go with me" (vs. 8) and Deborah answered, "Very well. . .I will go with you. But you will receive no honor in this venture, for the LORD's victory over Sisera will be at the hands of a woman." So she accompanied Barak (vs. 9).

When Sisera heard that the Israelites were revolting, he mobilized 900 iron chariots and all his army and went to the Kishon River. Deborah told Barak, "Get ready. . . . For the LORD is marching ahead of you" (Judges 4:14 NLT). So Barak and his warriors rushed into battle. Apparently, at that exact moment, God sent an earthquake, because "the earth trembled" and "the mountains quaked." Awestruck, Sisera's army panicked. Then "the cloudy skies poured down rain," and "the Kishon River swept them away"

(Judges 4:14; 5:4, 21 NLT).

Barak was willing to lead untrained farmers against a professional army and iron chariots, but he wanted to be sure God was with him. He also wanted to know exactly when to send his men into battle. If Deborah being with him guaranteed success, Barak didn't mind that she got credit for winning the battle. Many men today could learn from this example.

As Christians, we're aware that "there is no longer . . . male and female. For you are all one in Christ Jesus" (Galatians 3:28 NLT). But many men still have a problem with God using women, even though He is able to help them accomplish great things. However, women, like men, can become discouraged. Wonder Woman had lived for untold centuries, but at the end of World War I in 1918, she practically gave up on fallen humanity. As she tells Bruce Wayne, "A hundred years ago I walked away from mankind—from a century of horrors."[150] This is described in the 2017 movie, *Wonder Woman*, which from the trailer, promises to be a fascinating story.

When you're young and full of energy and idealism, you often attempt great, daring things. But quite likely you also make mistakes, rub people the wrong way, and are misunderstood. So you may end up minding your own business and playing it safe. It's good to learn prudence and wisdom as you age, but don't withdraw completely from the world. People still need heroes, and heroines, who can rise up in God's time, anointed by His Spirit, and do wonders.

53. RUNNING THE RACE

David wrote about the splendor of sunrise, saying that the sun "rejoices like a great athlete eager to run the race" (Psalm 19:5 NLT). Young men and women who are fast, and who *know* they're fast, are excited to race. It gives them a tremendous rush—all the more so if by doing it they're fulfilling their calling in life. The Christian athlete, Eric Liddell, who won the men's 400 meters at the 1924 Summer Olympics in Paris, said, "I believe God made me. . .fast. And when I run I feel His pleasure."[151]

The Flash is one of DC Comics' greatest superheroes. He has already appeared in two TV series, and will star in his own movie in 2018. Barry Allen (the Flash's actual name), who worked in the Criminal and Forensic Science

Division of the Police Department of Central City, gained his powers when he was doused by a mixture of chemicals and struck by lightning. Barry soon found that he could run, think, and react at super speed. He was a blur to his enemies, if they could see him at all. As the Flash, he also had incredible endurance that allowed him to run great distances.

Marvel Comics also has a super speedster, a mutant named Quicksilver (Pietro Maximoff). He appeared in the movies *Days of Future Past* and *Apocalypse*, as well as in *Age of Ultron*. The first movie gives viewers an excellent idea of the things a superhero who is super-fast can accomplish. They can nudge bullets to the side so they miss their targets, they can check people's ID and return it to their wallets so quickly that the people aren't even aware that they've moved, and they can vibrate at such an accelerated rate that they shatter the thickest glass.

The idea of being so fast that one's movements are undetectable, of being able to do something so quickly that no one can stop you or even know what you've done, is very appealing. If moving at such speed were real, it would give people tremendous control over many life situations. The Flash used his powers for good, but in *Days of Future Past*, Quicksilver mainly used his speed to pull off petty theft.

There were many speedy men in Bible times. The swiftest were chosen as runners to carry important news, especially during times of battle (see 2 Samuel 18:19–32). "Asahel was as fleet-footed as a wild gazelle" (2 Samuel 2:18 NIV), but in his case, speed by itself wasn't enough; he met his death while pursuing the mighty warrior Abner.

And then there were men who were supernaturally empowered with speed. The prophet Elijah wasn't normally very fast, but God miraculously enabled him to outrun King Ahab's chariot. One day, when he was leaving Mount Carmel, "Ahab rode off to Jezreel. The power of the LORD came on Elijah and, tucking his cloak into his belt, he ran ahead of Ahab all the way to Jezreel" (1 Kings 18:45–46 NIV). Elijah was more than just *fast* that day. This was a tremendous marathon: Jezreel was 30 miles away from Carmel.

But being fast and strong are only two aspects of good running. The New Testament lays out three other principles key to success. First, the book of Hebrews urges us to "throw off everything that hinders and the sin that so easily entangles. And let us run with perseverance the race marked out for us" (Hebrews 12:1 NIV). In New Testament times, Olympic runners often trained with weights strapped to their bodies to strengthen them and increase their endurance. When it came time for the race, they discarded the weights and ran swiftly and light of foot. The apostle Paul likened such weights to sin and bad habits, and said to "throw off everything" that weighs you down and holds you back.

Second: the racecourse, like the Christian life, is clearly marked out, and to win you have to stay inside the lines and not run out of bounds or take shortcuts. Paul wrote, "Anyone who competes as an athlete does not receive the victor's crown except by competing according to the rules" (2 Timothy 2:5 NIV). In life, people commonly cut corners and cheat to get ahead, but as a Christian you are called to compete according to the rules.

Third, you have to persevere. You cannot slack off, stop by the side of the road, and fall asleep like the speedy Hare, who ended up losing the race to the slow but tenacious Tortoise. At the end of his life of faithful service to God, Paul was able to say, "I have fought the good fight, I have *finished the race*, I have kept the faith" (2 Timothy 4:7 NIV, emphasis added). He then eagerly looked forward to receiving the prize, which God, the righteous judge, would give him. Being fast like the Flash or the Hare is good, but you have to actually cross the finish line. To do that, you must persevere.

The Bible admonishes, "Run in such a way as to get the prize" (1 Corinthians 9:24 NIV). Are you doing that? As Eric Liddell's father, the Rev. J. D. Liddell, said, "Run in God's name and let the world stand back and in wonder."[152]

BATMAN

54. DECENT MEN IN AN
INDECENT TIME

When you think of the Batman movie *The Dark Knight* (2008), very likely the Joker, played by the brilliant, now-deceased actor Heath Ledger, immediately comes to mind. In fact, you could be forgiven for getting the impression that the Joker, not Batman, was the main character of the film. He always seemed in control, constantly projected an aura of fearlessness, had the best lines, and constantly kept one step ahead of his adversaries.

In *Batman Begins*, it is Bruce Wayne/Batman who projects a larger-than-life persona, who strikes fear into his enemies, and who can't be kept down. But in the second film, the Joker is continually outwitting Batman, who scrambles to keep up. In that movie, everything goes wrong for the good guys. Bruce's girlfriend, Rachel, rejects him so she can marry a handsome rival, Harvey Dent, Gotham City's district attorney. Then Rachel is murdered in a perverse, cruel trick. To top things off, Harvey is horribly disfigured in a fire, resulting in him giving himself completely over to evil. Then he too dies.

When Christopher Nolan and David Goyer began working on the new Batman trilogy, they were aware that previous Batman movies had lacked depth, so they strove for a darker, more realistic tone. Batman consequently became edgier and more brooding, and he was given a deep, gravelly voice. And he had a new, cruel side. He wasn't yet heating up the branding irons to mark screaming criminals, but he would soon be doing so.

This approach worked well in the first film, but following this line further took the second movie to a much darker place. After all, if courageous men like Bruce Wayne had fear, and noble heroes like Batman could be cruel, why not show that good doesn't always win, have psychotic killers cause suffering, and depict that righteous men can be twisted by tragedy and become evil? These may not lead to a satisfying, typical happy ending, but *do* they reflect real life—or *don't* they? The truth is, sometimes they do.

The Bible also doesn't hesitate to describe the darker sides and antiheroic actions of otherwise good men.

David is a classic example. He loved God passionately, courageously stood up for what was right, showed mercy to his persecutors, and wrote many inspired worship songs called psalms. God described David as "a man after his own heart" (1 Samuel 13:14 KJV), yet David lusted after another man's wife, committed adultery with her, and then had the man murdered. He then took this beautiful woman into his own bed permanently.

Batman was the Dark Knight, but he greatly admired Harvey Dent, calling him the "White Knight." This district attorney was a courageous, good man who was determined to better society. But then he was mutilated and went mad, and set out on a path of revenge, repeatedly flipping a coin to determine whether someone should live or die. Reflecting on why the Joker worked on twisting Dent toward evil, Batman declares, "You were the best of us. He wanted to prove that even someone as good as you could fall."[153]

That's precisely what the Joker had insisted: "You see, their morals, their code, it's a bad joke. Dropped at the first sign of trouble. . . . When the chips are down, these. . .these civilized people, they'll eat each other."[154] Typical of much the Joker said, this cynical statement is rooted in psychotic cruelty, but there's still some truth to it. Setbacks, pain, and tragedies have a way of savaging your nice Christian veneer and leaving your raw emotions exposed for everyone to see. Prolonged illness can sap your joy, and unrelenting grief can drain the hopeful attitude out of even the most optimistic people.

Suffering transformed Harvey into Two-Face, who tells Batman, "You thought we could be decent men in an indecent time! But you were wrong. The world is cruel. . . ."[155] Yes, the world *can* be cruel, and random violence, disease, and misfortune can strike any of us. But the Bible says, "Be not overcome of evil, but overcome evil with good" (Romans 12:21 KJV). And it further states, "Live clean, innocent lives as children of God, shining like bright lights in a world full of crooked and perverse people" (Philippians 2:15 NLT).

With God's help, you can rise above the darkness and the seemingly senseless and random cruelty of life. You don't have to give in to lust and selfishness when tempted, nor do you have to succumb to bitterness when you suffer. The apostle Peter tells us to consider Jesus' example: "When they hurled their insults at him, he did not retaliate; when he suffered, he made no threats" (1 Peter 2:23 NIV).

Yes, difficult as it may sometimes be, you can follow Jesus' example: "Consider him who endured such opposition from sinners, so that you will not grow weary and lose heart" (Hebrews 12:3 NIV). It may seem like you're losing, and you may actually *be* losing, but God will see to it that you're vindicated and rewarded in the end.

CATWOMAN

55. BEAUTY IS SKIN DEEP

In the comicbooks, many superheroines are depicted in skimpy outfits that reveal more skin than they cover, and many guys admit that they practically drool over the images. And even the movies that feature superheroines in full-body costumes often ensure that the outfits are so form-fitting that they highlight each voluptuous curve. And there's eye-candy for the women, too: nearly every Marvel movie features the obligatory scene of a shirtless superhero with an amazingly ripped torso. Actors like Chris Evans (Captain America) and Hugh Jackman (Wolverine) subject themselves to tough exercise regimes for months to be able to wow the ladies in these movies.

Now, there's nothing wrong with good-looking

actors and actresses having sex appeal. Nor is it wrong to appreciate that someone is easy on the eyes. Consider Sue Storm (played by Jessica Alba) in the movie *Fantastic Four*. Reed Richards exclaims "Wow!" upon seeing her, and she is disappointed when she realizes that he is in awe of the material itself, not her figure. But when the camera inordinately focuses on specific aspects of someone's body, it's no different than when beautiful women appear in teeny bikinis in car ads. It raises the age-old question, "What exactly are they selling here?"

The 2004 movie *Catwoman*, starring superstar Halle Berry, epitomizes all that is wrong with the sexualization of female protagonists. Not only did Catwoman barely resemble the standard Selina Kyle of the comics, but the constant sensual imagery betrayed the entire premise of the movie—a courageous female risking her life to expose a corrupt beauty industry.

In *Catwoman*, Patience Phillips works for a cosmetics company about to market a skin cream that miraculously reverses the ravages of aging. But then Patience happens to overhear a conversation describing the horrific health risks from prolonged use of the cream. When company big-wigs discover that Patience knows their terrible secret, the company's guards seek to kill her, eventually trapping and drowning her. But as she lay dead, washed up on the shore, a Mau cat, a messenger of the Egyptian goddess Bast, appears. Patience is given new life as a "catwoman" and is gifted with amazing speed, agility, and fighting abilities. She then embarks on a mission to find her killers and expose the company.

Apart from the strange nod to the cat goddess, this sounds like a worthwhile plot. But the sexualization of the heroine undermines it. Catwoman wears tight black leather leggings with little above the waist—basically only a skimpy bikini top barely adequate to contain her breasts. And Patience goes from being self-effacing to oozing with pride. When she is asked, "Catwoman. You *heard* of her?" Patience replies, referring to herself, "Oh yeah. . .hot. . . black leather. . .whip."[156]

The first *Fantastic Four* movie starts off with a noble theme as well, showing Susan Storm attempting to rekindle a failed romance with Reed Richards, the man she truly loves. And in the end of the story, Reed kneels and proposes to her, and she accepts. It is a truly biblical ending to their meant-to-be romance.

But again, there are flies in the ointment (see Ecclesiastes 10:1). The screenwriters seemed obsessed with the issue of Invisible Woman needing to disappear but her clothing not vanishing. How would she resolve this? Remove all her clothes, of course. They had her do *two* stripteases in the first movie, and a nude scene in the second. The first time, her brother Johnnie groans, "This is so *wrong*,"[157] and the second time, Sue asks, "*Why* does this always happen to me?"[158] By the third peep-show, viewers were asking the same thing. The answer was simple: the movie-makers were focusing on Alba's sex appeal long after it had gone from good taste to outright ogling.

Now, God Himself invented sex, and to make certain that men and women engaged in it, He created physical beauty and sex appeal as powerful stimuli to attract them to one another. One biblical love song tells a foreign princess that "the King will *greatly desire* your beauty" (Psalm 45:11 NKJV, emphasis added). But this uninhibited desire has its place—within marriage.

God recognizes that men and women greatly desire, and even need, intimate union, which is why Paul urged us, "To avoid fornication, let every man have his own wife, and let every woman have her own husband" (1 Corinthians 7:2 KJV). Solomon wrote, "May you rejoice in the wife of your youth. . . . May her breasts satisfy you always, may you ever be intoxicated with her love. . . . Why embrace the bosom of a wayward woman?" (Proverbs 5:18–20 NIV).

Beauty, after all, is only skin deep. Or, as the Bible says, "Charm is deceptive, and beauty is fleeting; but a woman who fears the LORD is to be praised" (Proverbs 31:30 NIV). There are tasteful ways to feature sexy women and buff men in the movies, even if Hollywood often doesn't want to bother to get it right.

GREEN LANTERN

56. A CHOSEN RINGBEARER

There is not just one Green Lantern, but an intergalactic police force called the Green Lantern Corps. They all wear a ring that allows them to draw on powerful energy. When they wear the Power Ring, it creates whatever object they imagine out of green, glowing energy.

The founders of the Green Lantern Corps divided the universe into 3,600 regions and then sent a Power Ring to each region, where each ring chose a bearer. One of the criteria for being a ring-bearer was that he be without fear. In the beginning of the 2011 movie *Green Lantern*, Abin Sur, the Green Lantern of Sector 2814, is attacked by a powerful foe named Parallax. Abin Sur crash-lands on Earth and, knowing that he is dying, instructs his ring to find a worthy successor. The ring chose Hal Jordan.

Each ring must be periodically recharged by a lantern-like artifact. While it's recharging, the Green Lantern repeats, "In brightest day, in blackest night, no evil shall escape my sight. Let those who worship evil's might, beware of my power, Green Lantern's light."[159] When speaking this oath, Hal is transported to the planet Oa. There he undergoes training and meets corps leader Sinestro, who, noting that Hal has fear, tells him that he is unworthy to bear the ring.

But another Green Lantern, Tomar-Re, has more confidence in the ring's wisdom and says, "The ring chose you. It wouldn't have done so if it hadn't seen something in you." He adds, "The ring never makes a mistake." Discouraged, Hal replies, "This time it did."[160] And as long as he believes that, he lacks the confidence to fulfill his mission. However, a friend named Carol Ferris assures him that although he isn't fearless, the ring saw that he has the ability to overcome fear.[161]

And he does. Hal perseveres and eventually conquers Parallax without the help of the other Green Lanterns. After his victory, he is highly honored.

You may have felt similar discouragement when attempting to fulfill a job God has called you to. Perhaps you have a special talent, and God has lined you up with the ideal assignment. But if you mess up or fall short of expectations, both you and others may begin to wonder if you really *are* the right person for the job. It's even worse when you fail because of bad moral choices.

Green Lantern's ring is a powerful symbol. In biblical times kings wore a precious ring engraved with royal designs that was called a "signet" ring because it was used to "sign" royal documents. After an edict was written on a clay tablet, the king would press his ring into the clay, authorizing it. If the edict was written on papyrus and sealed shut with wax, the king would press his ring into the nearly cooled wax.

When a king highly favored and trusted someone, he would hand that person his ring. King Xerxes did this with a Jew named Mordecai: "The king took off his signet ring . . .and gave it to Mordecai," telling him and Esther, "You yourselves write a decree. . .as you please, in the king's name, and seal it with the king's signet ring" (Esther 8:2, 8 NKJV). God even compared people to such a ring. He told one ruler, "I will take you, Zerubbabel. . .and will make you like a signet ring; for I have chosen you" (Haggai 2:23 NKJV).

But even highly honored people, if they fall into sin and fail to repent, can lose their position and power. This happened to King Jehoiachin, to whom God said, "I will abandon you, Jehoiachin. . . . Even if you were the signet ring on my right hand, I would pull you off" (Jeremiah 22:24 NLT).

God has promised a unique, heavenly crown to those who serve Him well. Peter told Christians who set an example for other believers, "You will receive the crown of glory that will never fade away" (1 Peter 5:4 NIV). This "crown of glory" is *separate* from "the crown of life which the Lord has promised to those who love Him" (James 1:12 NKJV). The crown of life is your salvation and is undeserved. The crown of life is given to *all* believers, and no one can take it from you. The crown of glory, however, can be lost. Unlike the crown of life, you *can* allow others to take this crown from you. How? By failing to fulfill what God has called you to do. Jesus said, "Hold on to what you have, so that no one will take away your crown" (Revelation 3:11 NLT).

If the Lord has given you an assignment and you fail to do it, He will find someone else. . .and that person will receive the reward He had intended for you. So be faithful to obey God and fulfill your calling. And be sure not to lose a glorious crown out of a sense of unworthiness or fear. These heavenly rewards are worth fighting for.

SHAZAM

57. STRENGTH TO OVERCOME

Shazam was the most popular superhero of the 1940s, selling more comicbooks than even Superman. A young boy named Billy Batson would shout, "Shazam!" and would immediately be struck by a bolt of magical lightning, which transformed him into a super-powerful adult. (He used to be called "Captain Marvel," but since Marvel Comics has a character by that name, DC's superhero was renamed "Shazam," after the dying wizard who chose Billy as his replacement.) In the newest comicbooks, he's a troubled 15-year-old foster child.

Shazam is an acronym for the entities who gave Billy his great powers: Solomon, Hercules, Atlas, Zeus, Achilles, and Mercury. Billy has vast wisdom and knowledge like

Solomon. Hercules gives him superhuman strength. Atlas grants him the stamina to endure physical assaults and to heal quickly. Zeus hurls the thunderbolt that transforms him into a superhero and helps him resist magical attacks. Shazam has the courage and fighting skills of Achilles, and Mercury enables him to fly and run at superhuman speed.

With so much going for him, with so much power under the hood, it might be easy to imagine that Shazam never has a bad day, that he would always beat his enemies and always be victorious. No wonder young boys run around exclaiming, "Shazam!" and even Peter Parker utters "Shazam!" when trying to shoot his spider web.[162] In *Spider-Man 2*, he asks Aunt May about his comicbook collection, so it's a safe bet that he had Shazam comics among them.

Like Billy Batson, most people wish that they could shout one word and instantly receive all the wisdom, power, and courage that they need to face life's problems. Many people, in fact, secretly wonder why God *doesn't* provide such power. (I say "secretly" because they usually realize that such an attitude is unrealistic. Still, it doesn't stop them from wishing.)

God *does* make a great change in your life the instant the Spirit of Christ enters your heart. The Bible says, "If anyone is in Christ, he is a new creation; old things have passed away; behold, all things have become new" (2 Corinthians 5:17 NKJV). But the full transformation takes a lifetime, and it involves daily abiding in Him, staying close to Him, and being constantly renewed by His Spirit.

Shazam dwells in a magical refuge called the Rock of Eternity, and he is literally one with the Rock—so much so that he can only be away from it for 24 hours at a time. But God is *our* Rock of Eternity. The Bible says, "The LORD is my rock and my fortress and my deliverer" (Psalm 18:2 NKJV) and "The LORD has been my defense, and my God the rock of my refuge" (Psalm 94:22 NKJV). God is "a shelter from the wind and a refuge from the storm. . . and the shadow of a great rock in a thirsty land" (Isaiah 32:2 NIV). We too should not go long without drawing close to Him in prayer.

Just as Shazam is one with the Rock of Eternity, Christians are one with God: "He who is joined to the Lord is one spirit with Him" (1 Corinthians 6:17 NKJV). If you're a believer, the Spirit of Christ lives within you (Galatians 4:6). Jesus said, "Abide in Me, and I in you" (John 15:4 NKJV). Jesus lives in you, but you must also live continually in Him. This means seeking Him in prayer and staying close to Him by obeying Him.

It's ironic that Achilles is one of the heroes empowering Shazam, because Achilles was famous for one weakness.

According to Greek myths, his mother Thetis dipped him in the river Styx to make him invulnerable, and every part of his body was bathed in the river, except for the heel by which she held him. As an adult, he was killed by a poisoned arrow striking that heel. Because of that, the phrase "Achilles' heel" refers to a weakness in an otherwise strong hero that can lead to downfall. Shazam's major weakness was that he was a proud, immature teenager. It's easy to understand how this could cause problems.

There is an underground chamber in the Rock where seven statues stand as reminders of the Seven Deadly Enemies of Man that motivate the villains Shazam battles. But Billy Batson himself is not immune to their influence. These enemies are Pride, Greed, Selfishness, Envy, Injustice, Hatred, and Laziness. These statues are a close copy of the Seven Deadly Sins—also known as the cardinal vices—of the Catholic Church: pride, greed, lust, envy, gluttony, wrath, and sloth.

If God has given you great power, talent, or influence to use for His glory, be aware of weaknesses that could potentially undermine your life for Him and bring you down. As the ancient maxim says, "Know thyself." Then make sure to "know the LORD" (Hosea 6:3 KJV). He alone can strengthen your spirit, help steel your resolve, and enable you to overcome. As the Bible tells us, "The people who know their God shall be strong, and carry out great exploits" (Daniel 11:32 NKJV).

JOKER AND HARLEY QUINN

58. EMULATING THE BEST

Too many movies go all-out with big-name actors and spectacular special effects but leave viewers unimpressed because they lack a good plot. *The Suicide Squad* became famous for its very scattered plot. Some movies even have a riveting storyline but fail because they emphasize profanity, violence, and gore. And some movies leave a sour taste on our tongues because of an even deeper problem—the entire moral premise is off.

Depicting self-obsessed or evil "heroes" and glorifying cruelty and violence is a growing trend in superhero movies, but this is the first movie with an entire cast of villains as dark anti-heroes fighting an even *worse* group of villains. The Comics Code Authority came into being because of just such issues in the late 1940s and early 1950s. The resultant "Code for Editorial Matter," Part A, point 5 stated: "Criminals shall not be presented so as to be rendered glamorous or to occupy a position which creates the desire for emulation." Point 6 added, "In every instance good shall triumph over evil and the criminal punished for his misdeeds."[163]

But in recent years, most comicbook companies have abandoned the Code as obsolete. Comic and movie producers were weary of always-heroic heroes who sometimes came across as wooden and two-dimensional. And good triumphing over evil "in every instance" was frankly unrealistic. So they began to emphasize edgier, less virtuous protagonists.

In 2016, *The Suicide Squad* hit the theaters, where it received generally negative reviews from critics. It featured some of DC's worst villains in what is arguably the worst superhero movie to date. Not even the psychotic love relationship between Joker and Harley Quinn could salvage it. In the film, a secret government agency called ARGUS creates a team named Task Force X, which is made up of the worst of the worst, and sends it on dangerous missions in exchange for shorter prison terms. There is constant risk of death in these black ops, which is why they're nicknamed The Suicide Squad. Amanda Waller, head of ARGUS, tells a military officer, "I want to assemble a task force of the most dangerous people on the planet. . ." Surprised, the officer states that these are bad guys. Amanda replies, "Exactly. And if anything goes wrong, we blame them."[164]

This group of villains includes criminals such as Harley Quinn, the Enchantress, Captain Boomerang, Tattooed Man, Killer Croc, Deadshot, Slipknot, and El Diablo. The officer's big question is, "What makes you think you can control them?"[165] Waller's confident answer is that she is able to motivate people to act against their own self-interest. She simply had explosives implanted in their bodies to deter them from going AWOL.

A number of soldiers in past wars were lawless men. Some redeemed themselves through selfless acts and heroism, but others proved they were incorrigible by committing war crimes. The Suicide Squad is reminiscent of some of David's warriors. When King Saul was hunting David, many virtuous warriors joined him. But a number of lowlifes also followed him: "Everyone who was in distress, and everyone who was in debt, and everyone who was discontented gathered to him; and he became captain over them" (1 Samuel 22:2 NASB). A later verse describes "all the wicked and worthless men among those who went with David" (1 Samuel 30:22 NASB).

David realized that such warriors were a liability, so he eventually sent them away, saying, "I hate all who deal crookedly; I will have nothing to do with them. . . . I will not tolerate people who slander their neighbors. I will not endure conceit and pride. I will search for faithful people to be my companions. Only those who are above reproach will be allowed to serve me. I will not allow deceivers to serve in my house" (Psalm 101:3, 5–7 NLT).

Movies like *Suicide Squad* leave you with mixed emotions: Normally, you at least enjoy the realistic acting, the gripping plot, and the special effects of superhero movies. *Suicide Squad* had few redeeming qualities. But even in the movies that do, something about them disturbs you. When movies portray cruel, evil people as cool and "create the desire for emulation," you feel like you're being sold a bad bill of goods.

The Bible tells us, "Whatever is true, whatever is noble, whatever is right, whatever is pure, whatever is lovely, whatever is admirable—if anything is excellent or praiseworthy—think about such things" (Philippians 4:8 NIV), and commands, "Beloved, do not imitate what is evil, but what is good" (3 John 1:11 NASB), adding, "Remember your leaders, who spoke the word of God to you. Consider the outcome of their way of life and imitate their faith" (Hebrews 13:7 NIV).

You must be sensitive to God's Spirit when He gives you a sense of unease that certain movies, books, or video games are "off." David stated, "I will refuse to look at anything vile and vulgar. . . . I will reject perverse ideas and stay away from every evil" (Psalm 101:3–4 NLT). *Suicide Squad* may have been a big-budget movie with lots of action and explosions, but it failed to deliver in very basic ways.

BATMAN AND SUPERMAN

59. HOPE AND JUSTICE

If you have any doubts that DC Comics has entered an age of dark and troubled superheroes, just take a look at *Batman v Superman: Dawn of Justice*. In this movie, Batman is driven by bitterness over his parents' murders and hopelessness over the death of his (Bruce Wayne's) employees during Superman's battle with Zog. The former Batman trilogy had seen him becoming darker and more menacing, and this movie explores a cynical, jaded superhero well past his expiry date.

Batman despondently preaches, "I bet your parents taught you that you mean something, that you're here for a reason. My parents taught me a different lesson, dying in the gutter for no reason at all."[166] The lesson he got from this? There is no meaning in life apart from the one you hammer out of it with your bare fists.

This movie is titled *Dawn of Justice*, but having lost faith in justice, the once-idealistic crime-fighter degenerates into a cruel vigilante, so cruel that he begins marking his enemies with a searing-hot brand. It was as if he is declaring, "This brand is my signature, my declaration that I'm taking matters into my own hands because I've lost faith in due process of law." He continues branding men even after he learns that other prisoners murdered those who were marked.

Batman even fashions a spear—a primitive, brute-force symbol of slaughter—with which to kill Superman. He argues that even if there is even the smallest possibility that the super-powered alien is a menace to humanity, that he has to be preemptively destroyed. Lex Luthor and Batman are *both* driven to kill Superman, and they battle over possession of the Kryptonite that would help them do it. In past years, it was the bad guys who used Kryptonite for murderous purposes, but in this movie the line between heroes and villains is greatly blurred.

Small wonder that Superman observes, "No one stays good in this world."[167] And if you give up hope, that's true. You take on a cynical mindset and are ruled by your suspicions. You become merciless. Bruce Wayne and Lex Luthor gave up hope and idealism over personal tragedy—Bruce when his parents were murdered in a botched holdup, and Lex when the God he had once believed in didn't protect him from an abusive father.

Now, you shouldn't be naive; you must take precautions to protect yourself from those who would victimize or defraud you, and that includes knowing whom to trust, locking your doors, and standing up for your basic rights. But you are also to live with the knowledge that though this life is often *not* fair, you can trust God to administer justice in the next life: "Let them that suffer according to the will of God commit the keeping of their souls to him in well doing, as unto a faithful Creator" (1 Peter 4:19 KJV).

Contrary to Batman's grim pronouncement, you *do* mean something, and you *are* here for a reason. Life isn't just a senseless collection of pain and grief. God knows that you will often suffer setbacks, misfortunes, and injustice, yet He calls you to live by a higher code. After listing many troubles that beset Christians, Paul wrote, "In all these things we are more than conquerors through Him who loved us" (Romans 8:37 NKJV). Even though at times you seem to be losing, victory will eventually be yours.

Batman slugging it out with Superman made for a terrific gladiatorial fight, but you may have wondered why the moviemakers contrived to pit them against *each other* instead of against a world filled with villains. But though it seemed like a mere plot device, the fact is, good friends *do* have fallouts. Misunderstandings happen, people say and do thoughtless things, and those they hurt often *do* refuse to forgive.

Worse yet, malicious busybodies sometimes deliberately pit friends against one another. Lex Luthor admitted that he had worked to turn Batman and Superman against each other—and this happens all too often in real life. Solomon warned, "A perverse man sows strife, and a whisperer separates the best of friends" (Proverbs 16:28 NKJV). When Saul was hunting David, Saul was driven by his own paranoia, but he was also egged on by wicked advisors. That is why David asked him, "Why do you listen to the words of men who say, 'Indeed David seeks your harm'?" (1 Samuel 24:9 NKJV).

It took Superman sacrificing himself to destroy the monster Doomsday for Batman to wake up. After the Man of Steel died, Bruce Wayne confessed to Diana, "I've failed him . . .in life. I won't fail him in death."[168] How had he failed him? By indulging in mistrust and suspicion. By being so set against Superman that he was willing to believe anything negative about him. And once he became convinced that Superman was a threat, he felt justified in trying to execute him.

May you never give up hope in justice or rush to judge others.

WHAT ABOUT YOU?

60. ARE YOU A TRUE BELIEVER?

Why do we have such a love for superheroes? Why do we find comicbooks about their adventures so appealing, and why do untold millions of fans flock to see the latest superhero movies? Sure, the films are action-packed and filled with astonishing special effects, and sometimes they have great plots. But there are more primal reasons, the main one being that they tap into a deep need and fear.

People fear many things in the world around them. Evil often seems to be lurking in the shadows. This is why believers pray that angels will stand guard around them to protect them. The Bible states clearly that "angels. . .are stronger and more powerful" than mere mortals (2 Peter 2:11 NIV), and promises, "The angel of the LORD encamps around those who fear him, and he delivers them" (Psalm 34:7 NIV). You may envision angels as having blond hair and fluffy wings, but it's more accurate to picture them as super-powered heroic beings living in another dimension.

We also long for heroes because many terrifying things happen in the world, things completely beyond our control. Crimes take place around us, ominous conspiracies threaten, and things generally seem hell-bent for destruction. Whether it's a train derailment or a terrorist threat, an illness or an accident, we feel helpless to deal with dangers that assail our personal world. Deep down, we long for a hero, someone more than human, to arise, stand between us and the evil, and save us.

In the Bible, God often sent other powerful heroes to rescue His people—Gideon, Jephthah, Samson, Jonathan, and David, to name just a few: "In the time of their trouble, when they cried to You, You heard from heaven; and according to Your abundant mercies You gave them deliverers who saved them from the hand of their enemies" (Nehemiah 9:27 NKJV). David was called "the man exalted by the Most High, the man anointed by the God of Jacob, the hero of Israel's songs" (2 Samuel 23:1 NIV). Many of these heroes in the Bible had such great power that they could literally be called *super*heroes.

Like the ancient Jews, we today wait for the powerful Messiah to rise and deliver us from our enemies. And the good news is: God has sent the Messiah, His only Son, Jesus—and He comes to the rescue of those who trust in Him and wait for Him. The apostle Paul put it well when he wrote, "Christ Jesus came into the world to save sinners" (1 Timothy 1:15 NIV). He not only saves us from the ultimate danger of eternal death, but as we cry out to Him, He also saves us from danger and evil in our daily lives.

Are you a true believer? Have you put your faith in Jesus Christ, the Son of God? The Bible tells us, "Anyone who believes in God's Son has eternal life" (John 3:36 NLT) and "he is able, once and forever, to save those who come to God through him" (Hebrews 7:25 NLT). If you believe that Jesus died on the Cross for your sins and was resurrected from the dead, you're saved. God then sends the Spirit of His Son into your heart (Galatians 4:6) and He literally lives inside you.

If you've never prayed and asked Christ to come into your life, do it now. You can pray a prayer similar to this: "Dear God, I believe that Jesus Christ is Your Son, that He died on the Cross to pay the penalty for my sins, and that He was buried and raised from the dead on the third day. I ask You now to forgive my sins and to send the Spirit of Your Son into my heart. Fill me with Your Holy Spirit so that I may have the strength to obey you. In Jesus' name, I pray. Amen."

If you're a true believer and worship Jesus as your

Lord, your life will start to show clear evidence of the transformation that He brings in you. Then you too can be heroic. Most modern superheroes have outstanding powers that set them apart from the rest of us, and while we're incapable of such spectacular feats, we can nevertheless relate to their courage, perseverance, and self-sacrifice. As Aunt May said about Spider-Man, "[We] need a hero—courageous, self-sacrificing people, setting examples for all of us."[169]

With God's Spirit living inside you, you too can be empowered and be a hero. You may not *feel* like much of a hero, but neither did Peter Parker before he was bitten by a spider, or the Fantastic Four before they were exposed to gamma rays, or Green Lantern before he put on the power ring. With God's Spirit in you, you have *great* power. Jesus promised that "you will receive power when the Holy Spirit comes upon you" (Acts 1:8 NLT). And remember: "You are of God, little children, and have overcome them, because He who is in you is greater than he who is in the world" (1 John 4:4 NKJV).

ENDNOTES

1 http://collider.com/captain-america-civil-war-trailer-easter-eggs-joe-anthony-russo/ accessed November 25, 2015

2 Code of the Comics Magazine Association of America Inc. Adopted on October 26, 1954

3 Fantastic Four #72, March 1968

4 Dr. Strange issue 13, April 1976

5 The Mighty Thor Annual #14, November 1989

6 Warlock Chronicles #2, August 1993

7 Doctor Strange Vol. 2, No. 13, April 1976

8 The movie, *Avengers: Age of Ultron* (2015)

9 The movie, *Guardians of the Galaxy* (2014)

10 The movie, *Captain America: The First Avenger* (2011)

11 The movie, *The Avengers* (2012)

12 The movie, *Captain America: The First Avenger* (2011)

13 Ibid

14 The movie, *The Avengers* (2012)

15 The Ultimates 2 Volume 1: Gods and Monsters (2005)

16 The movie, *Avengers: Age of Ultron* (2015)

17 The movie, *Thor: The Dark World* (2013)

18 The movie, *Spider-Man* (2002)

19 The Amazing Spider-Man, no. 1 (1963)

20 The Mighty Avengers Special No. 5 (1972)

21 https://en.wikipedia.org/wiki/Robert_Downey,_Jr., accessed Nov. 23, 2015

22 The movie, *The Avengers* (2012)

23 The movie, *Iron Man* (2008)

24 The movie, *Iron Man 2* (2010)

25 The movie, *Iron Man 3* (2013)

26 Ibid

27 The movie, *The Incredible Hulk* (2008)

28 The movie, *Thor* (2011)

29 The movie, *The Avengers* (2012)

30 The movie, *Thor* (2011)

31 The movie, *The Avengers* (2012)

32 The Mighty Thor Annual no. 14, November 1989

33 The movie, *Thor: The Dark World* (2013)

34 The movie, *Captain America: The Winter Soldier* (2014)

35 Ibid

36 Ibid

37 The movie, *The Avengers* (2012)

38 Ibid

39 Ibid

40 The movie, *Iron Man 2* (2010)

41 Ibid

42 Ibid

43 The movie, *Avengers: Age of Ultron* (2015)

44 Ibid

45 The movie, *The Avengers* (2012)

46 Ibid

47 Captain America no.117 (1969)

48 The movie, *Captain America: The Winter Soldier* (2014)

49 The movie, *Ant-Man* (2015)

50 The movie, *Avengers: Age of Ultron* (2015)

51 Ibid

52 Ibid

53 The movie, *X-Men: The Last Stand* (2006)

54 The movie, *X-Men* (2000)

55 Ibid

56 Ibid

57 The movie, *X-Men: The Last Stand* (2006)

58 Ibid

59 Ibid

60 Ibid

61 Ibid

62 The movie, *X2: X-Men United* (2003)

63 The movie, *X-Men* (2000)

64 The movie, *X-Men Origins: Wolverine* (2009)

65 The movie, *X-Men* (2000)

66 The movie, *X2: X-Men United* (2003)

67 The movie, *X-Men* (2000)

68 Ibid

69 The movie, *X-Men: The Last Stand* (2006)

70 The movie, *X2: X-Men United* (2003)

71 The movie, *X-Men: The Last Stand* (2006)

72 The movie, *X-Men* (2000)

73 The movie, *X-Men: The Last Stand* (2006)

74 Ibid

75 The movie, *Avengers: Age of Ultron* (2015)

76 The movie, *X-Men: First Class* (2011)

77 The movie, *Captain America: Civil War* (2016)

78 The movie, *Batman Begins* (2005)

79 The movie, *Spider-Man 3* (2007)

80 Ibid

81 Ibid

82 The movie, *Fantastic Four: The Rise of the Silver Surfer* (2007)

83 The movie, *Fantastic Four* (2005)

84 Ibid

85 The Infinity Crusade: *Enlightenment*, Vol. 1, No. 2 (July, 1993)

86 The movie, *Fantastic Four* (2005)

87 Ibid

88 The movie, *Fantastic Four: The Rise of the Silver Surfer* (2007)

89 The Infinity Crusade: *Enlightenment*, Vol. 1, No. 2 (July 1993)

90 The movie, *Fantastic Four* (2005)

91 Ibid

92 Ibid

93 Fantastic Four, Vol. 3, No. 56 (August, 2002)

94 The movie, *Fantastic Four* (2005)

95 Silver Surfer, vol. 1, no. 1 (August, 1968)

96 Silver Surfer, vol. 1, no. 3 (December, 1968)

97 Ibid

98 Daredevil, vol. 7, no. 12

99 Daredevil: Guardian Devil, vol. 2, no. 8

100 Daredevil, vol. 5, no. 10

101 Warlock Chronicles #2, August 1993

102 Walker, Karen (June 2009), "The Life and Death (and Life and Death) of Adam Warlock" (TwoMorrows Publishing) 34: 3

103 The movie, *Iron Man 3* (2013)

104 The movie, *Thor: The Dark World* (2013)

105 The movie, *X-Men Origins: Wolverine* (2009)

106 Ibid

107 Ibid

108 The movie, *Guardians of the Galaxy* (2014)

109 The movie, *Deadpool* (2016)

110 Ibid

111 The movie, *The Avengers* (2012)

112 The movie, *Avengers: Age of Ultron* (2015)

113 The Ultimates 2 Volume 1: Gods and Monsters (2005)

114 The movie, *Daredevil* (2003)

115 The Amazing Spider-Man, vol. 2, issue no. 46, pgs 6-8 (December, 2002)

116 The Amazing Spider-Man, vol. 2, issue no. 53, page 6 (July, 2003)

117 The movie, *X-Men* (2000)

118 The movie, *X-Men: First Class* (2011)

119 The movie, *X-Men* (2000)

120 Ibid

121 The movie, *The Avengers* (2012)

122 Ibid

123 Ibid

124 The movie, *Avengers: Age of Ultron* (2015)

125 The movie, *Captain America: Civil War* (2016)

126 The movie, *Avengers: Age of Ultron* (2015)

127 The movie, *X-Men Origins: Wolverine* (2009)

128 The movie, *Thor: The Dark World* (2013)

129 Ibid

130 Silver Surfer, vol. 1, no. 3 (December, 1968)

131 Ibid

132 Ibid

133 The movie trailer, *X-Men: Apocalypse* (2016)

134 Ibid

135 The Infinity Crusade: *Enlightenment*, Vol. 1, No. 2 (July 1993)

136 Ibid

137 Ibid

138 Ibid

139 The movie, *Ghost Rider* (2007)

140 The movie, *RoboCop* (2014)

141 Ibid

142 Ibid

143 The movie, *Man of Steel* (2013)

144 Ibid

145 Ibid

146 Ibid

147 The movie, *Batman Begins* (2005)

148 Ibid

149 The movie, *Batman vs. Superman: Dawn of Justice* (2016)

150 Ibid

151 The movie, *Chariots of Fire* (1981)

152 Ibid

153 The movie, *The Dark Knight* (2008)

154 Ibid

155 Ibid

156 The movie, *Catwoman* (2004)

157 The movie, *Fantastic Four* (2005)

158 Ibid

159 The movie, *Green Lantern* (2011)

160 Ibid

161 Ibid

162 The movie, *Spider-Man* (2002)

163 Code of the Comics Magazine Association of America Inc. Adopted on October 26, 1954

164 The movie trailer, *Suicide Squad* (2016)

165 Ibid

166 The movie, *Batman vs. Superman: Dawn of Justice*

167 Ibid

168 Ibid

169 The movie, *Spider-Man 2* (2004)

ABOUT THE AUTHOR

Ed Strauss is a freelance writer living in British Columbia, Canada. He has authored or coauthored more than fifty books for children, tweens, and adults. Ed has a passion for Biblical apologetics and besides writing for Barbour, has been published by Zondervan, Tyndale, Moody, and Focus on the Family.

Love Sports and the Outdoors?
Check Out. . .

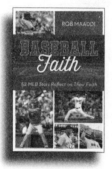

Baseball Faith by Rob Maaddi

Baseball Faith will inspire and encourage readers in their faith journey, as 52 MLB players—past and present—share their stories and how they are chasing the success that only comes from being God's man and following His plan. Featuring personal stories from Hall of Famer John Smoltz, three-time Cy Young Award winner Clayton Kershaw, former MVP Albert Pujols, perennial All-Star Mariano Rivera, and many more.

Paperback / 978-1-68322-094-7 / $16.99

The Man Minute by Jason Cruise

Every "Man Minute" devotional is designed to be read in sixty seconds, yet a man will carry the insights he gleans into a lifelong journey of spiritual manhood. *The Man Minute* is packaged alongside a DVD featuring hunts—each couched in spiritual truths—with some of the most recognized hunters on the planet.

Hardback / 978-1-63058-718-5 / $16.99